Napoleon

Napoleon

John Bowle

Introduction by Elizabeth Longford

Follett Publishing Company Chicago

To Felix Markham, *doyen* of Napoleonic studies

© George Weidenfeld and Nicolson Limited
and Book Club Associates 1973

First published in the
United States of America
1975 by
Follett Publishing Company,
Chicago

ISBN 0–695–80543–6
Library of Congress Catalog Card Number
74–21373

Printed in England

House editor Jenny Ashby
Art editor Andrew Shoolbred
Layout by Juanita Grout

Contents

Introduction

To use the language of the examination papers, some great lives are 'optional'. Napoleon's life is a 'must'. He rightly saw himself as a Man of Destiny. At his zenith, his imagination soared beyond Europe into the still unexplored treasure-house of America and Aladdin's cave in the East. If his despotic predecessor, Louis XIV, could say *'L'Etat c'est moi'* – 'I am the State' – Napoleon Bonaparte was to see himself as the Universe.

French youth today, it is rumoured, have at last shaken themselves free from the Napoleon legend. If that is so, this is the moment to see how it all happened. John Bowle here presents the thunderous story against an awe-inspiring background of Toynbee-esque proportions, but delightfully fretted with flashes of irony. After reading it, we may wonder whether young or old can ever quite escape from the thrall of genius which was at once so tyrannical and so human.

Turning first to Napoleon's human side, some may be surprised that John Bowle labels Napoleon's attitude to women 'matter-of-fact'. On reflection, however, it is clear that this supreme ruler was indeed ruled by the facts. He could be infatuated with Josephine; but when the facts dictated the foundation of a dynasty rather than a reputation for constancy, he obeyed. Divorcing the now barren Josephine, he married – the Austrian Empire. His passion for the actress Mademoiselle Georges had been so tumultuous that once during a *rendezvous* in his palace he collapsed in her arms at dead of night in a faint. It was she who was blamed and banned from the Tuileries. No wonder she called Wellington 'much stronger'. Napoleon was a romantic, but about himself. He behaved with women in the spirit of a sultan not a troubadour.

Napoleon's vision of world government was no mean one. It might have been splendid, had he not placed himself so arrogantly at the centre. With his efficient police and gagged Press, John Bowle unhesitatingly calls him the first of the modern dictators. Against his brilliant administrative reforms must be set his loathing for the masses. The 'citizens' of the Revolution became 'subjects' of the Empire, as John Bowle reminds us. There can be nothing but thankfulness for Waterloo. Nevertheless, so compel-

7

ling was the Emperor's magnetism that English Whigs considered Europe fortunate to be in such rapacious hands and under such heavy boots. They wept when he abdicated, sent him presents and beautified their houses with his bust.

Today we can only marvel as Napoleon fights out Waterloo over again on St Helena, spilling rivers of ink instead of blood and emerging virtually the victor. Like all modern dictators, his pen was mighty as his sword. More potent still was the pathos of his end. A real-life Prometheus, he lay chained to his South Atlantic rock, while the looted clock of Frederick the Great ticked away the long hours and the vultures of boredom and hereditary disease pecked out his guts. 'I don't want to end my destiny in sands and deserts,' he had said eleven years earlier. His mirage, at any rate, has not dissolved.

Elizabeth Longford

War makes rattling good history, but Peace is poor reading. So I back Bonaparte for the reason that he will give pleasure to posterity.

SPIRIT SINISTER IN *The Dynasts* BY
THOMAS HARDY

1 The Man of Destiny

When Napoleon wanted to bring Europe into an association
of States (the only human being who was strong enough
therefor) they botched everything with their 'Wars of
Liberation' …
NIETZSCHE

England has saved herself by her exertions; and will,
as I trust, save Europe by her example
WILLIAM PITT

'NEVER', WROTE NELSON IN 1805, in the summer before his death at Trafalgar, 'was the probability of universal monarchy more nearly realized than in the person of the Corsican.' Universal monarchy? It was a fantastic ambition; yet Napoleon attempted it. Western Europeans were then attaining the mastery of the world, and the conquest and unification of Europe might well have given the victor the mastery of the Americas, of Eurasia and of Africa. The Napoleonic wars were the first contest for *Weltmacht*.

Yet Napoleon failed; and failed just because of this expansion of Europe, for he provoked an unprecedented and extra-European resistance which drew both on the sea-borne wealth derived, under the protection of the Royal Navy, by the British from the Industrial Revolution of which they were the pioneers, and from the man-power and vast territories of Russia. Like the leaders of Germany in the world wars of our own time, he was overwhelmed on two fronts, oceanic and Eurasian.

But he nearly brought it off, and if ever there was a 'Man of Destiny', it was Napoleon. For such a man must be a genius, able to ride and even sometimes to direct the storms which are his opportunity and of which he is himself the daemonic emanation. He was of the eighteenth century, rooted in the old regime, the last of the 'enlightened' despots; he was also the first dictator of modern times, borne up on the tides of popular will, relying on police control, on propaganda, plebiscite and psychological warfare. He was a Voltairean rationalist and agnostic in the eighteenth-century style, but also a romantic of insatiable ambition, his monstrous self-dramatization a projection of an imaginative inner world; a Machiavellian realist, yet carried away by the bogus romance of Macpherson's *Ossian*. He was, after all, the contemporary both of Bentham, the rationalist 'improver' with his abstract view of man, and of Beethoven, the greatest romantic composer. He was very well read and had early absorbed Plato's *Republic* and Plutarch's *Lives*; a considerable writer and a brilliant conversationalist with a memorable terse power of phrase. Compared with Napoleon, the proletarian tyrants of the twentieth century, with a more comprehensive power, are sub-men risen from the gutter, figures of a more sinister and barbaric devastation.

Though he held power only for fifteen years, Napoleon altered the face of Europe. As Baldwin ruefully complained of Lloyd George, he was 'that terrible thing, a dynamic force', who, according to another critic, went through life with 'as much consideration as a cactus hedge'. But he was creative as well as

PREVIOUS PAGES Horace Vernet's impression of the Emperor Napoleon reviewing troops at the Tuileries.

12

destructive. He is comparable to Alexander, the conqueror whom he most admired, who Hellenized the Near East and left behind him the rich Hellenistic kingdoms and the tradition of Empire assimilated by Rome; to Julius Caesar who extended a Mediterranean power beyond the Alps over the Gauls to the Atlantic; to Augustus who stabilized the Roman Empire which under Hadrian would extend from the Euphrates to Scotland. He also has affinities with Constantine, who, anxious for divine favour, grasped the political potential of Christianity and, determined that Graeco-Roman civilization should turn Christian, convoked the great Councils of the Church and shifted the centre of gravity of the Roman Empire to the more defensible East, so that it lasted until the fifteenth century and brought western Russia into Christendom. Napoleon's edifice proved ephemeral, but his indirect influence would be incalculably pervasive, for he carried with him the force and confidence of French civilization and the egalitarian principles of the Revolution. He claimed to be the heir of Charlemagne, who had drawn the political outlines of eastern and central Europe, and revived the Holy Roman Empire in the West to whose dilapidated remnant Napoleon would put an end. The Hapsburg Charles v, though he ruled large areas of Europe and overseas territories much vaster than ever did Napoleon, was laboriously on the defensive, and Louis xiv's objectives are limited and conventional when related to the eagle vision of the Corsican adventurer. Alexander probably remains the European most nearly to compare with him.

But Napoleon's historical and technological context was very different from that of classical antiquity, the Middle Ages or even early modern times. As a military genius, he exploited a new kind of warfare based on improved eighteenth-century techniques in fire-power and organization, and he restored the war of movement, as in the twentieth century the invention of the tank broke the stalemate of trench warfare. Most decisively, he achieved an overwhelming concentration of force at the critical place by massed concentrations of artillery; for Napoleon was originally a 'gunner' who took his first chance at the siege of Toulon, and whose first decisive political intervention came with a 'whiff of grapeshot'. But he was also a master of strategy and bold improvisation who could hold in mind the picture of far-flung battle and confusion on a scale hitherto unknown, and take calculated risks in handling the mobile divisions of huge armies. Cromwell was an amateur to him; he fought with armies of at most about

ABOVE *'Le maquis fleuri',* or wild scrubland,
to which Corsicans retreated in times of danger.
LEFT Maison Milelli, the birthplace and home
of Napoleon at Ajaccio on the island of Corsica.

twenty thousand men; Napoleon took 450,000 men into Russia, though not so many came out. He was also adept in political warfare, knowing just when to time a military or political stroke, with the instinct for showmanship apparent in Alexander, Caesar and Constantine, who all created their own legends and commanded loyalty by a calculated charisma.

Yet, though he well knew that 'all depended on the army', Napoleon was also a devastatingly intelligent statesman; always, until his brief decline, objective. He saw essentials with a rather appalling lucidity; no mere military dictator but a great civilian politician and administrator. He brought order into the chaos of Revolutionary France, swept away the debris of the *ancien régime*, rationalized the administration and the law and designed to spread his reforms over all his Empire.

In the eyes of the Radicals, he betrayed the Revolution (revolutions are always betrayed) and, as a true Machiavellian, he used the Catholic Church, in whose dogmas he disbelieved, to manage the mass of the people for whom he had a realist's contempt. 'Men must be very bad', he remarked, 'to be as bad as I think they are.'

Moreover, Napoleon was not a Frenchman. He was an emanci-

16

pated Corsican with an intense loyalty to the metropolitan culture to which he owed his career. As Hitler was Austrian and Stalin Georgian, Napoleon, too, was an outsider; and he viewed both the French and all the subjects of his brief Empire with a certain detachment. And, knowing this, he must always have had at the back of his mind the thought of his formidable mother as expressed in her Corsican accent – *'pourvu que ça doure'* – 'so long as this lasts'. He was a cosmopolitan European who projected a great imperial palace on the Capitol, never achieved, and who called his son the King of Rome.

Apart from his violent passion and swift disillusionment over Joséphine de Beauharnais, his first wife, his adventures with women were matter-of-fact, and his way of life relatively frugal and austere. He cared little about food or drink; not for him the orgies of Asian conquerors, though he too came to be thought a 'scourge of God'. He arranged his life with military precision and routine and he was a tiger for work. Save on official occasions, he was indifferent to dress and deliberately wore a simple uniform, in contrast to the flamboyant finery of his parvenu marshals. His charm, when he switched it on, was apparently irresistible; as when he got round his insular British captors on HMS *Bellerophon*, and the British oligarchy had to take care that he should not meet and hypnotize the susceptible Prince Regent. This fascination briefly won over the neurotic Tsar Alexander Pávlovich, and still worked on the soldiers who intercepted him on the Route des Alpes after he had landed at Antibes, impatient of a humdrum and penurious exile on Elba. 'Come, kill your Emperor', he said, 'if you will.' No one fired; they flocked round him shouting *'Vive l'Empereur!'*. They had been softened up by propaganda, and Napoleon had fifteen hundred peasantry at his back as well as his following from Elba, but he knew his Frenchmen. With hard-drilled Prussians or an English battalion impervious to heroics, his chances might not have been so good.

In spite of the vast documentation of Napoleonic scholarship, no one can know the inner mind of this extraordinary man. He had a passion for efficiency; flung himself into the grand design and detail of administrative and legal reform; took account of economic problems according to his lights; fought a losing battle with the Catholic Church over secular schools and state-controlled higher education; supervised the Press; bought up able men by the 'Legion of Honour' and the pensions that went with its awards; collected – or plundered – works of art from most of Europe to adorn Paris – a Renaissance prince in the manner of his Italian origins.

But he wanted more than efficiency – he wanted adventure. When still a political general, not content with the traditional French objectives in Italy, he had the ambition to descend upon Egypt with an entourage of civilian experts, who were to lay the foundations of Egyptology and reveal to the Egyptians their own past, long overlayed with a decadent Turko-Mamelūk regime. Here, like the thirteenth-century Frederick II of Hohenstaufen who, though excommunicated, won Jerusalem by diplomacy, he even pretended to turn Muslim for political ends. For he meant to strike at the British through subverting their rule in India from the base of a permanent French colony in Egypt.

As his power grew, these vast ambitions mounted until the final grandiose and impossible commitments; a gruelling war in Spain draining the resources of his armies, and the colossal gamble of invading Russia. For he may have believed that if the Tsar could be brought to terms, as he had been at Tilsit, they could again enforce the boycott and blockade of Great Britain and might even combine to master central Asia and break the British hold on India; a project likely to appeal to the visionary Tsar, whatever Napoleon's own reservations. Had he got away to the Americas, his exploits in Latin America might have surpassed Bolívar's, though after the first glamour, his stock might soon have fallen in the mainly Anglo-Saxon United States.

But there was one aspect of warfare that Napoleon never fully understood. A 'land animal', like Stalin, he expected impossibilities of his admirals: nor were they in a position to take risks, for although the design of the best French battleships was unsurpassed, the morale and leadership of the fleets had been undermined by the Revolution, while over the years the British blockade had diminished French training at sea. The British admirals, with an imperturbable grasp of oceanic strategy backed by the implacable resolve of an oligarchy and nation fighting for their lives, had tactical superiority as well. For Nelson's revolutionary tactics were to break the enemies' line, rather than run parallel to them in an inconclusive slogging match, and as the great ships slowly passed their opponents they raked them fore and aft with the new carronades, causing appalling casualties right down the ship.

At the battle of the Nile, Nelson's calculated risk came off, and superior British seamanship so manœuvred the ships that the

Napoleon in the military uniform of the *chasseur de la garde*: a painting by R. Lefebvre.

French fleet were caught between a cross-fire that annihilated them. And again at Trafalgar, the British had complete mastery. So Napoleon, the potential world conqueror, was caged in Europe, and the long attempt to bring the British down by economic blockade and boycott brought his vast but precarious military empire to spreading conflict and collapse. For, when all is said and done, Napoleon was a tyrant. An enlightened despot, indeed, but one whose rule was based on battle and devastation, on wars which cost the lives of more than four hundred thousand Frenchmen and an incalculable number of their opponents, and which left a tradition of military aggression and 'glory' which would work like a virus in Europe until it broke out again in the great wars of 1870, 1914-18 and 1939-45 which led to Europe's catastrophe and eclipse.

'The Emperor is mad', once remarked one of his generals; and

20

in a sense he was – in that his ambitions had become unlimited. The creative egotism of genius had become the inhuman and colossal egotism of unbridled public power, and the old medieval doctrine that a tyrant was the enemy of the human race had been vindicated. For no one, however brilliant and many-sided his genius, untiring his abilities and hypnotic his private and public charm, can withstand the corruption of unbridled power. The best biography of Adolf Hitler (that by Alan Bullock of 1952) is sub-titled *A Study in Tyranny*, and although Napoleon was in contrast an enlightened despot, so that, as Geyl writes, 'one almost feels that one should ask the pardon of his shade for mentioning his name in one breath with the other', a just account of him must follow the same analysis.

And for all his impatience of muddle and archaism, Napoleon never transcended his origins. Like most men, with age he reverted to them. He had the Duc d'Enghien, who was innocent of conspiracy, kidnapped and murdered, and he left a legacy to a would-be assassin of Wellington. To the English oligarchy he was the 'grand Disturber'; to the general public he was 'Boney' – a rather ridiculous if very dangerous foreigner. He was, of course, both above and below their conventions: a man of Olympian view; in his despotic way, a good European; but ruthless and treacherous as are all power addicts and, though one of the most creative and brilliant of the men of destiny, he came to his reckoning.

By modern standards, it was not too hard – a long frustration and decline at St Helena. Hitler committed suicide and his henchmen were executed. Napoleon, thanks in part to his own psychological skill, became a legend of perennial fascination.

We must not leave this world without leaving traces which remind posterity of us.
NAPOLEON

2 The Climb to Fortune 1769-96

WITH HIS OLIVE SKIN AND CLASSIC PROFILE, Napoleon was a Mediterranean man: for the first time since antiquity and its aftermath Europe was overrun by an adventurer from the south. His father came of a noble Tuscan family, whose ancestor Ugo 'Buona Parte' had taken the name in commitment to the 'good' Ghibelline (imperialist) faction in Florence. Here, in the late twelfth century, he had been a Councillor; but he had been forced out to settle at Sarzana near La Spezia, whence in the sixteenth century Francesco Buona Parte migrated to Corsica. His descendants had been lawyers and officials, and Carlo-Maria Buona Parte had read law at the University of Pisa; his brother, Lucciano, was Archdeacon of Ajaccio.

At eighteen, Carlo, a handsome, charming, rather improvident youth, had married Maria Letizia Ramolino, then fourteen. She was a beautiful and determined girl, little more than five feet tall, whose ancestors had been related to the influential Coll' Alto family in Lombardy but had long been settled in Corsica. Her father had been commander of the garrison in Ajaccio and Inspector of Roads and Bridges under the Genoese – a position that can hardly have given him much scope.

Carlo had been an ardent and active supporter of Boswell's hero Paoli in the resistance to the Genoese. Had he still followed Paoli, Napoleon might have entered the British Army when in 1768 the Genoese had sold Corsica to the French. But after Paoli had fled to England, Carlo had come to terms with the new masters. Napoleon's father, a freethinker with a considerable library, looked to France and French civilization; his mother, a handsome, formidable and grasping little matriarch who bore fourteen children of whom eight survived, remained resolutely Corsican, frugal and *dévote*.

Corsica at that time was a world in itself, archaic, gloomy, beautiful and undeveloped. In the 1830s, Prosper Mérimée thus described Ajaccio, Napoleon's birthplace,

The appearance of the town increased the impression caused by the solitude of its surroundings. There was no movement in the streets, when one only met a few idle figures and always the same ones. There were no women, except a few peasant women, come in to sell their produce. One heard no one speak loudly, laugh or sing, as in the Italian towns.

It was a sombre country, with its own austere and mountainous quality, in spring the scent of the *maquis* perceptible well out to sea. Life was poor and harsh, though there was plenty of

goat-cheese, fish, olive oil and game in the mountains: roads were atrocious and the grim traditions of the vendetta still compulsive. It had been only in 1768, before Napoleon's birth on 15 August 1769, that France had effectively taken over the island. At first, like Paoli, the Buona Partes had taken to the *maquis*, and Letizia had been traipsing about the mountains in the months before Napoleon's birth. But after Carlo-Maria had gone over to the French, he soon secured a judicial post in Ajaccio. He was thus early recognized as a member of the French *noblesse* – an honorary Frenchman – and he dressed accordingly, with powdered wig and sword. He was also able to enter his sons Giuseppe and Napoleone at the French academy at Autun, at the suggestion and with the help of the Comte de Marbœuf, the French Governor and Commander in Corsica, who was much taken with Madame Buona Parte.

But before this turning point in the boys' lives is followed up, the rest of the family demand consideration: like the children of the contending Augusti and Caesars of the times of Diocletian and Constantine, some would become important pieces in a far-flung dynastic power-game and be promoted to a fantastic but precarious eminence in a European Empire. They were not, on

Napoleon's parents: his father, Carlo-Maria Buona Parte (*right*) and his mother, Maria Letizia Ramolino (*left*). They provided the French-Corsican background which determined Napoleon's ambitions and his character.

Two of Napoleon's sisters: Eliza (*top*) and Pauline (*above*).

the whole, much help to him and often a grave liability; indeed, he once remarked that they behaved as if he had mismanaged their father's inheritance. Besides Giuseppe and Napoleone, the family included Lucciano, Luigi and Jerome, and their sisters Eliza, Pauletta and Maria Annunziata or Caroline: the prospects of all of them were bleak. They were people of some consequence in Ajaccio, poor but proud; but though uncle Lucciano might boast that the Buona Partes had never paid for corn, wine or oil, Carlo's property was only a large house in Ajaccio, which he shared with his uncle and some cousins, a farm and a couple of vineyards, and his wife had brought him no more than about thirty acres and a small mill. Although, in the Mediterranean way, the Italian-speaking children had plenty of company, they were brought up hard; and in 1776 Carlo had to obtain a certificate that he had not the means to educate his sons. He even had to borrow the money to take Giuseppe and Napoleone to France.

From these straitened beginnings, vast prospects would open out. The formidable matriarch would be transformed into Madame Mère, installed in a palace with a fortune of a million francs. But she remained grasping and provident, always putting by: 'I've got seven or eight Kings', she once said, 'who will one of these days fall back on me.' And they did. She ended in pious and grand seclusion in Rome, having substantially helped them, and still with a considerable fortune. She outlived Napoleon by fifteen years.

The others were less helpful. Giuseppe (Joseph) married Julie Clary, a rich bourgeoise girl from Marseilles, with whose sister, Eugénie Désirée, Napoleon briefly fell in love. She eventually married Marshal Bernadotte and became Queen of Sweden. In 1806 Joseph became King of Naples and two years later he was transferred to the august monarchy of Spain, to be ignominiously ejected in 1813. After Napoleon's fall, he took refuge in the United States, but returned to die in 1844 in Florence. He was the one who looked most like Napoleon, but had little of his drive and less of his austerity.

Lucciano (Lucien) debarred by his eye-sight from the army, was the most radical and rhetorical, and politically he played briefly the most crucial part; for when President of the Five Hundred on the eve of the *coup d'état* of *Brumaire* (22 October – 20 November 1799, according to the Revolutionary system of months decreed by the National Convention in 1793, the months following the seasons of the year), he saved Napoleon from being outlawed by the enraged deputies, and brought in the Directorial guard by telling them that the General had been threatened with stilettos. After this essential service, Lucien, who married twice for inclination, refused to play the dynastic game by marrying the Infanta of Spain, and retired, as the Prince of Canino, to Italy. Then, attempting to reach the United States, he was captured by the British and put out to grass in Gloucestershire, where he wrote an epic on *Charlemagne*. In the end, he returned to Italy and died in 1840 at Viterbo.

Luigi (Louis), one of Napoleon's staff in Egypt, was forced to marry Hortense de Beauharnais, the General's step-daughter, whom he detested, for his inclinations lay in another direction. In 1806 he was made King of Holland, but soon took the side of the Dutch. Two years later he abdicated, and returned to Italy where, an amiable man of letters, he died at Livorno in 1846. But dynastically he was the most important, for his reputed son, Louis Napoleon, would become Emperor of the French (from 1852, as Napoleon III).

Jerome, the youngest, was to witness this event. He was the longest lived, the most military and the most flamboyant and he at first served in the navy, but in 1803 jumped ship and married the daughter of a Baltimore businessman. Napoleon refused to receive her, but Jerome fought at Jena and in 1807 was made King of Westphalia. Early in the Russian campaign, he was superseded in command and retired to sulk in his kingdom, but he fought at Waterloo. Then he retired to Italy and survived to become a Marshal of France and President of the Senate under Napoleon III. He died in France in 1860.

Napoleon's sisters were all spirited but even more difficult. Eliza married a Corsican and in 1809 became Grand Duchess of Tuscany; she was capable but treacherous, and intrigued with her brother-in-law Murat in his doubtful designs to create a kingdom in Italy. She ended up in Trieste as the Contessa de Compignano. Pauletta (Pauline) was the most attractive: her first husband, General Leclerc, one of Napoleon's staff, died in the West Indies, and she married the Prince Borghese; but he did not suffice. She was a woman of taste, but her escapades created scandal in Paris and Rome. She died in 1825 in Florence. Caroline was the youngest, cleverest and most ambitious, a chip of the old block: 'Whenever I meet her', Napoleon remarked, 'I have to fight a battle.' She married Joachim Murat, the Marshal whom Napoleon described as incomparable in battle and a fool in politics, and who, in 1806, succeeded Joseph as King of Naples. Urged on by Caroline to retain and even enlarge his kingdom, he intrigued after Leipzig with the Austrians for a guarantee for Naples. But with the Bourbons set for reinstatement, it was quite unreliable; and after Napoleon's return from Elba, Murat double-crossed the Austrians and tried to raise a nationalist revolt in Italy. It failed; Murat rejoined Napoleon, who rejected him, and then escaped to Corsica. Following Napoleon's example, he then invaded his former kingdom with a handful of men, but was at once taken and shot in Calabria. Caroline retired with her four children to Florence.

After his marriage with Joséphine de Beauharnais, Napoleon also acquired two step-children, Eugène and Hortense. Of Eugène, alone of all his relations, Napoleon would say 'he never caused me any strife'; he turned out to be a good general and a tactful and competent Viceroy of Italy, married the Princess Auguste Amelie, daughter of King Max Joseph of Bavaria, became Duke of Leuchtenberg and Prince of Eichstatt, and died at forty-three at his villa near Lake Constanz in 1824. His descendants would marry into the Romanov and Bernadotte families. Hortense would become Queen of Holland and Duchess of St Leu; she remained loyal to Napoleon after his final abdication, and entertained him at Malmaison, the house she had inherited from Josephine; her son, Charles Louis Bonaparte, would become the Emperor Napoleon III.

Such were the Buona Parte and Beauharnais families which, in clannish Corsican style, Napoleon sought to organize and thrust ahead. And though, as ruler of France, he was careful to exclude the claims of a horde of cousins and collaterals, his dynastic policy would suffer when he exalted his brothers and sisters regardless of the feelings of the royalties or the peoples concerned.

In 1779 Carlo Buona Parte took his two elder boys to France where, through the favour of the Comte de Marbœuf, a place had been found for Napoleone, now aged nine and still speaking Corsican Italian, in one of the royal military schools lately founded for the sons of the nobility. It was at Brienne in Champagne in north-eastern France, in a climate and surroundings very different from Ajaccio: and as a preliminary breaking-in, both Joseph – who was destined for the priesthood though he refused to enter it – and Napoleon, as they were now called, were brought to Autun, high in the wooded hills of Burgundy, where the cathedral of St Lazare contains some of the most elaborate and peculiar medieval sculpture in France. After four months at the excellent cathedral school, Napoleon was ready for Brienne, where he remained until 1784.

He was subjected to the ragging generally accorded to anyone unusual and of outlandish accent and origins, but he quickly mastered French, his strength of personality was early apparent and his sufferings have been exaggerated. He won enough authority to direct mock battles in the snow, and afterwards showered favours on his masters and contemporaries. As a child, he may have hankered for Corsica, but his loneliness was soon merged in his daemonic instinct for domination. He read widely in history, but his *forte* was mathematics and though, like all his brothers save Jerome, he was a natural writer and enjoyed music, his interests were practical and austere. He was no omniverous *beau sabreur*, and frowned on the sexual and convivial peccadillos of his colleagues.

Nominated as a royal scholar among the hundred and fifty aristocratic cadets of the much grander *École Militaire* in Paris, he was assigned to the artillery. Here he met boys of more distinguished family and here, though some looked down upon him as a scholar, he shared a lavish way of life in a metropolitan setting. There was ample leave and a habit of taking privilege for granted. Here his gift for mathematics found fuller scope, and in September 1785, after only one year, he passed out forty-second out of fifty-eight, a remarkable if not an outstanding result after so short a preparation.

That year was a turning-point. A project for entering the navy, even at a pinch the British navy, had been early abandoned, and now he was comissioned as a second lieutenant of artillery in the regiment of La Fère, with a blue uniform with red facings: in a modest way, he had arrived. That year his father had died and Napoleon, at sixteen, now became in effect head of the family. So, posted in January 1786 to Valence-sur-Rhône in the Dauphiné, he returned that September to deal with his family's affairs in Ajaccio; after seven years, he had forgotten the dialect, but he was still a Corsican patriot. Transferred to Auxonne in Burgundy in 1789, the year of the Revolution, he dealt faithfully with local food riots, but in September he was again in Corsica, where the Revolution had opened prospects of a liberal regime. He organized a national guard, and saw himself as a liberator; but the conservative Paoli was still the national hero.

29

Napoleon the Soldier in Youth

It was perhaps inevitable that Napoleon, the son of an active member of the resistance to the Genoese led by Paoli, should be marked out for a military career. His father, looking towards France, secured for him a place at the royal military school at Brienne, from which he progressed as a royal scholar to the Ecole Militaire in Paris.

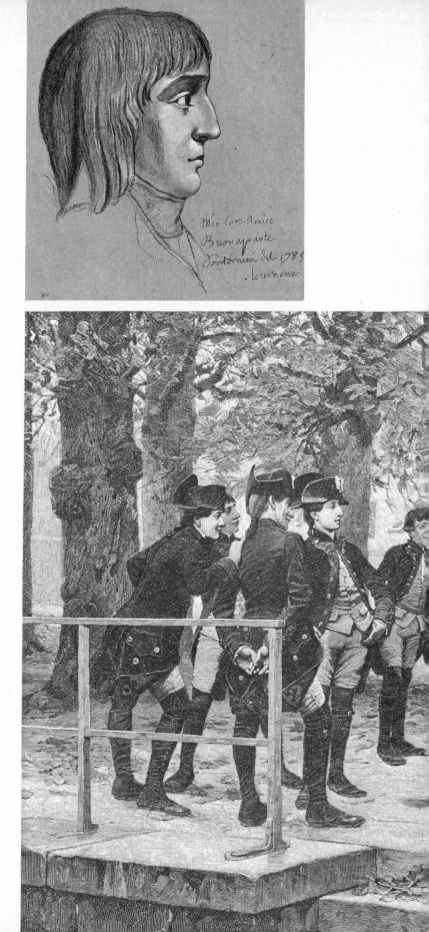

ABOVE A view of the Ecole Militaire in Paris.

ABOVE LEFT A portrait of Napoleon aged sixteen, sketched in crayon by one of his friends and the earliest known impression of him.

LEFT Other pupils at Brienne make fun of the novice Bonaparte.

Napoleon returned to Valence, yet his mind was still on Corsica; early in the following year he got himself posted back as adjutant-major to a battalion of the local national guard, and soon by intrigue and violence got himself elected lieutenant-colonel. But Paoli and his faction detested the Revolution, and when at Easter 1792 Napoleon fired on a clerically-sponsored procession, he incurred a dangerous vendetta. Having now made Corsica too hot to hold him, he returned to Paris, and none too soon for he had been struck off the army list for not reporting to his regiment by April. But he soon made his peace with the authorities, and during the summer he witnessed the first crisis of the Revolution – the collapse of the monarchy, the attack on the Tuileries and the September massacres. He always considered that the Tuileries had fallen through the incompetence and irresolution of the King; already disillusioned by Corsican politics, he now took the measure of those at the top in Paris and of the Parisian populace as well. He felt equal contempt for both.

But that September he took no part in the decisive battle of Valmy, won mainly by the French artillery. His fixation on Corsica remained; and he got the Girondin government to approve an attempt to seize the strategic islands of Caprera and Maddalena off the north-east coast of Sardinia, commanding the Straits of Bonifaccio. The expedition, under a Paolist commander and based on Ajaccio, was a fiasco; the Paolist and pro-French factions were soon at each other's throats and the Paolists proclaimed that all the Buona Partes were 'derived from the slime of despotism' and condemned to 'perpetual execration and infamy'. Letizia and the rest of the family took to the *maquis*, to be rescued from the shore by Napoleon and Joseph in a French ship. Paoli now invited the British to occupy the island, and the Buona Partes took refuge in penury at Marseilles. Here Joseph opportunely married Julie Clary, and Napoleon fell in love with her sister, Eugénie Désirée. But her father decided that 'one Buona Parte' in the family was enough.

Dismal as appeared the prospects of the Buona Partes in Marseilles, it was the darkest hour before the dawn. Napoleon's fixation on Corsica was over – he would not end up as a Corsican party boss or by a bullet in the *maquis*. Better prospects were opening, for in 1793 the French republic was in mortal danger from foreign attack. The Convention which, under Danton's leadership, had proclaimed the republic, was no longer representative, if it ever had been, and had driven their own General

ABOVE One of Napoleon's early loves: Eugénie Désirée Clary, painted by Gérard.

OPPOSITE A contemporary print of cameos showing the various members of the Bonaparte 'Imperial Family'.

FAMILLE IMPÉRIALE.

MARIE-LOUISE, IMPÉRATRICE. NAPOLÉON, EMPEREUR. JOSÉPHINE, IMPÉRATRICE.

NAPOLÉON, DUC DE REICHSTADT. LA PRINCESSE PAULINE. JÉRÔME BONAPARTE. LA PRINCESSE ELISA.

LA REINE CAROLINE. JOSEPH BONAPARTE. LA REINE HORTENSE. LUCIEN BONAPARTE.

LOUIS BONAPARTE. LAETITIA BONAPARTE. EUGÈNE BEAUHARNAIS.

Propriété de l'Éditeur. (Déposé.)   A ÉPINAL, CHEZ PELLERIN, IMPRIMEUR - LIBRAIRE.

The mob storms the
Tuileries in September 1792.

Dumouriez to go over to the enemy and to call them 'three
hundred scoundrels and four hundred imbeciles'. The moderate
Girondins had failed to save the king, and so alienated middling
opinion, while Danton had gone over to the more radical politicians
who would send him to the guillotine.

After the defeat of the Prussians at Valmy, the French armies
had overrun the Austrian Netherlands (Belgium), much of the
Rhineland, Savoy and Nice; all superficial conquests and dangerous commitments. Appalled at the threat to the old European
order, the Dutch and the Spaniards had now entered the war,
and then the British, determined to prevent a French stranglehold
on Antwerp and the mouth of the Scheldt. Save for a brief interval
of cold war following the Peace of Amiens (1802-3), the British

34

would remain implacable in their determination to prevent Napoleon's domination of the continent and the threat that he might outbuild their fleet. In the end, their wealth, sea-power and tenacity would bring Napoleon down.

The republic was thus confronted with an alliance of Prussia and Austria and of the greatest sea-power in Europe. A Committee of Public Safety was formed, a Jacobin dictatorship of the Left dominated by the fanatical Robespierre, ruthless, secret and centralized. Like Lenin, Robespierre ruled by terror; he killed Danton, and sent hundreds of opponents to the guillotine; controlled the armies by political commissioners; decreed a *levée en masse*; sent the armies against provincial revolts in La Vendée and Provence. And here was Napoleon's first chance: consigned to

35

routine duties at Nice and Avignon, under the command of General Carteaux, whose forces were putting down the revolt in Provence, Captain Bonaparte applied to be posted to the Army of the Rhine. And turning to political warfare, he wrote *Le Souper de Beaucaire*, a skilful polemic against the revolt in the Midi, and used part of a legacy from his uncle, the archdeacon, to print it.

It proved a good investment: he was now 'Citizen Bonaparte', a political partisan. Meanwhile, by July 1793, Carteaux, a flamboyant amateur soldier, formerly an artist, was besieging Toulon, where the British had reinforced the royalist insurrection. The artillery commander had been put out of action, and one of the government Commissioners, Saliceti, a Corsican of the pro-French faction, now put forward Napoleon's name. At a glance, he sized up the strategic essentials: the key to the harbour was the 'Little Gibraltar', the fort on the small peninsula that commands both the *petit* and *grand rades* of Toulon. This obvious fact had been lost on both civilian and military authorities, but so lucid and compelling was Napoleon's appreciation that his plan was sanctioned by the Paris government. By 17 December, after an assault of four days in pouring rain, the British were forced to evacuate the town and the magnificent harbours: Toulon surrendered. As second-in-command, Napoleon had served the guns and been bayoneted in the thigh by a British defender. He had shown his mettle: he was now 'somebody', at least in professional circles, and he was at once appointed a Brigadier General. He soon installed his family in a pleasant villa near Antibes.

Now it so chanced that the representative of the Jacobin government with the army of the south was Augustin, brother of Robespierre; perceiving Napoleon's ability, he ordered him to plan the strategy of an Italian campaign to strike at Austria through Italy, in conjunction with an offensive from the Rhine. And though in *Thermidor* (July) 1794, the fall and execution of Robespierre by politicians who restored a much more bourgeois interest, led to Napoleon's arrest and interrogation, he was reinstated on Saliceti's staff. But he was tarred with the Jacobin brush, and when Paoli handed over Corsica to the British, all Corsican officers were thought better away from the army of Italy; so the brilliant young staff officer was assigned to a command against the royalist rebels in La Vendée.

Napoleon refused to obey: he lingered in poverty in Paris, got appointed to the topographical branch of the service and carried on with his planning for the Italian campaign. Political influence

OPPOSITE Lethière's portrait of Joséphine de Beauharnais, who entered into marriage in a more calculating spirit than Napoleon.

37

The British and Spanish surrender to the French army at Toulon in December 1793.

had frustrated the War Office, so in August 1795 he was still precariously at the hub of affairs; and although he had provisionally accepted secondment to Turkey, with ambassadorial status and high pay, to organize the Sultan's artillery, the appointment was countermanded – a minor official in the War Office had decided that he was too good at topography to lose. So, retained as a planner for the war in Italy which was not going well, Napoleon was still in Paris for the political crisis that brought him to the centre of power and made him a famous political general – *Le Général Vendémiaire*.

38

After the fall of Robespierre, the Convention had devised a
new constitution: a Council of Five Hundred and a Council of
'*Anciens*', or Senate, along with an executive of five Directors in
theory elected by them. But the Directorate proved ineffectual:
detested by the *sans-culottes* and radicals, it was hated by the
Right; a royalist *coup* threatened and Paul de Barras, a Provençal
aristocrat who had fought in India, but was now a regicide, one
of the Directors, and the singularly corrupt politician who had
ably contrived the fall of Robespierre, was appointed to command
the Army of the Interior in Paris. He at once asked for Napoleon

as his second-in-command, and that night Napoleon made swift dispositions. When, the next day, 6 October or 14 *Vendémiaire* on the Republic's calendar, the insurgents attacked the Tuileries, this time the palace was much better defended.

A Captain Murat with two hundred cavalry had been detailed to secure and bring up forty guns and, 'a whiff of grapeshot' having killed thirty of the attackers, the counter-revolution in Paris collapsed: on Napoleon's orders the guns had fired case-shot, without warning, to kill. It had been a neat professional job; Napoleon was promoted major-general, then replaced Barras in the command of the Army of the Interior.

He also succeeded him in a more intimate way. Marie-Josèphe-Rose, Vicomtesse de Beauharnais, was a glamorous Creole from Martinique of a branch of the ancient family of Tascher de la Pagerie who owned a modest sugar plantation at Trois Ilets near Fort Royal. In 1794 Robespierre had guillotined her husband, Alexandre de Beauharnais. The well-to-do son of a former Governor of the French West Indies, he had thrown in his lot with the Revolution, been briefly President of the Constituent Assembly and then Commander-in-Chief of the Army of the Rhine. But he had failed to retrieve Mainz, and his aristocratic lineage had told against him. Josephine, though she had been

The 'whiff of grapeshot' which secured the collapse of the counter-revolution in Paris in October 1795 and led to Napoleon's promotion.

legally separated from him, had also been imprisoned; and would have suffered the same fate but for Robespierre's own execution and the disappearance of her dossier, purloined and eaten, as were many others, by the actor Delperch de la Bussière, who thus saved many lives. She was small, elegant, sympathetic, with chestnut brown hair and hazel eyes, and she had an intriguing West Indian lisp. In the general social collapse she had to fend for herself, and had become Barras's mistress.

The Government now called in all unauthorized weapons, and among them the sword of the late general, her husband. But Eugène, their handsome boy, now fourteen, was allowed to apply to the general officer commanding in Paris to get it back; and that officer was Napoleon. He cross-questioned Eugène and was favourably impressed; the boy wept and kissed the sword when it was returned. It had been a moving occasion, and Josephine felt obliged to call on the General to thank him herself. It was not long before she became his mistress and, what was more, his wife. Eugène and his sister Hortense would have their great careers.

Napoleon, with Mediterranean passion, had fallen madly in love. Josephine, though reckless about money, had been more calculating: she was deep in debt with an expensive household in the Rue Chantereine; she made a marriage of convenience, and within six months of it, in the general way of the Parisian political demi-monde of the time, she had cuckolded him. 'A thousand kisses', he would write, 'as ardent as you are cold.' 'He's a funny man, that Bonaparte', was all she said when he wrote from Italy accusing her of infidelity and threatening to kill himself. For all her languorous elegance and charm, she was hardly a reliable character, indolent and easy-going; and her noisy old pug Fortuné bit Napoleon in the leg when he was making love to her on their wedding night – 'a million kisses', he wrote from Italy, 'and even for Fortuné'. But their honeymoon was brief. Two days after their marriage, Napoleon left Paris; he had been appointed Commander-in-Chief of the Army of Italy. He was now twenty-six.

Caroline, sister of Napoleon (*top*) and her husband Joachim Murat (*above*). The portrait of Murat is by Gérard. The couple subsequently became King and Queen of Naples.

3 The Political General 1796-9

What have we to do with Destiny now? Politics is Destiny.

NAPOLEON

BY THE STANDARDS OF HIS TIME Napoleon was of medium height, well over five foot six; at this phase of his career, gaunt and predatory; still wearing an abbreviated pig-tail and long side-locks, 'with the profile of an eagle and the hairdo of a spaniel'. Though his chest was broad, he had small hands and feet and short legs; 'a lean sallow little man whose hat and boots seemed too large for him'. The Corsican Laura Permon, afterwards Duchesse d'Abrantès, whose widowed mother had refused to marry Napoleon, had nicknamed him 'Puss in Boots'. 'But there was in him a compact energy that made one think of a panther ready to leap rather than of a tomcat with odd sartorial tastes, and in the cold, calm gaze of his grey eyes there was a quality that inspired devotion in some, terror in all, and love in none.' With middle age and good living, he would become stout, with a rather greasy pallor, and with his dark brown hair, now receding, close cut, he would develop a consequential bearing and an abrupt and commanding style.

Such was the young Commander-in-Chief who in March 1796 arrived in Nice, bringing with him Louis Berthier, the Chief of Staff who would serve him until 1814. They worked well together: Berthier, though he became Prince of Wagram, was not so ambitious and jealous as most of the Marshals; he was already a mature professional who had fought in America, and he would remain within his indispensable role.

The lightning campaign soon began. Napoleon had about thirty-eight thousand men, ragged and ill-equipped but mobile – a revolutionary horde eager for plunder and to live off the country. He had had sacked five brigadiers and four cavalry colonels, brought in Murat and promoted Masséna, Augereau and Lannes. Then, sensing, as would Montgomery and his advisers at Alamein, that the juncture between discrepant allies was the place to strike, Napoleon went first for the Austrians, whom he had lured south through the Ligurian Alps by an advance on Albenga towards Savona along the coast, and at Montenotte and Millesimo and then at Dego, on the road from Acqui to Savona, he drove them back toward Alessandria, south-east of Turin. He then turned and routed the Piedmontese at Mondovi under the northern fringe of the mountains: 'Hannibal', he told his army, 'crossed the Alps: we have outflanked them.'

The Piedmontese now signed an armistice at Cherasco, giving Napoleon command of Cuneo so that the French could strike at

PREVIOUS PAGES Napoleon leads his troops across the bridge at Arcola in November 1796.

OPPOSITE ABOVE The capture of Alexandria by the French in July 1798 – a glorious start to an inglorious campaign. A contemporary print.
BELOW Napoleon's troops crossing Mont-St Bernard in May 1800

44

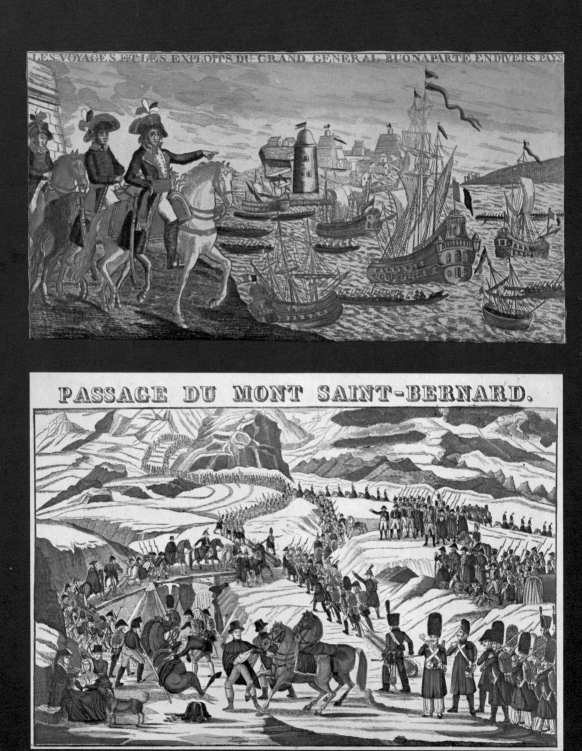

LES VOYAGES ET LES EXPLOITS DU GRAND GENERAL BUONAPARTE EN DIVERS PAYS

PASSAGE DU MONT SAINT-BERNARD.

'Puss-in-Boots': Napoleon
at the time of the campaigns
in Italy and Egypt.

once towards the Lombard plain. Napoleon's strategy became more
ambitious: it was nothing less than to destroy the Austrian armies
in Italy, cross the eastern Alps by the Brenner into Bavaria, or by
Villach and Klagenfurt on Vienna itself; while the French Army
of the Rhine, the northern half of a great pincer movement,
would strike into Bavaria towards the Danube. In the conditions
at that time, it was a wildly ambitious plan, and though Napoleon's
part of it was brilliantly executed, it was quite beyond the vision
of the civilian Directory in Paris, who were in great difficulties,
and who wanted simply to plunder Italy and then use it as a
bargaining counter over the Rhine.

Such was the speed of Napoleon's campaign that the Austrians were driven to retire on Mantua with its defensive marshes and lagoons; and the French, wheeling north-west, crossed the swiftly flowing Adda at the narrow wooden bridge at Lodi (the story that Napoleon led the rush over it is probably false) and captured Milan. So when, on 14 May, he entered the capital of Lombardy as a conqueror, he was already becoming a power in Europe in his own right: 'I had to act with *éclat*', he said, 'to win the trust and affection of the common soldier. I did so.'

In granting the armistice at Cherasco, Napoleon had already acted beyond his powers: 'After Lodi', he said later, 'I saw the world beneath me as if borne up on the winds.' The Directory, sensing that he had the bit between his teeth, now proposed to divide the command and appoint Kellerman, the victor of Valmy, in command in northern Italy and order Napoleon south to march on Genoa, Rome and Naples. Warned by his compatriot, Saliceti, whom he had thoughtfully put to handle the army funds, Napoleon wrote that if he had lost the confidence of the government he had better be employed elsewhere. The threat of resignation was decisive; the more so as the plunder of Italy was now pouring back into France

The Italian summer was now setting in, and the army of the Republic was battening on its plenty. The gaudy parvenu officers

Louis Berthier,
Napoleon's Chief of Staff.
He was eventually
to desert Napoleon.

47

were fêted in Milan; Napoleon, almost an independent pro-consul, began to regard himself, as he always would, more as a ruler than a general: doubtless he relished the sudden grandeur and affluence after the penury and uncertainties of his origins.

One thing only was missing: Josephine had not arrived. Napoleon had inundated her with letters, for he wanted total and reciprocal passion, and his love-letters make those of Henry VIII look sentimental and relatively chaste: the Corsican was more intimately anatomical. By July, after maddening delays, Josephine was at last installed in Milan; but Napoleon had to follow up the Austrians, and on her way to Italy his wife's eye had been caught by Hippolyte Charles, a charming young captain of Hussars. He proved not as unresponsive as his classical namesake, and he was a brilliant mimic and good company; once, when Napoleon, elated after a victory, returned unexpectedly to Milan, Josephine was on a jaunt with Charles to Genoa. 'I rush into your apartments', wrote her husband '... you are gone ... you are running after other amusements: you no longer care for your poor Napoleon.' *'J'arrive à Milan, je me précipite dans tes appartements ... tu n'y étais pas. Tu cours les villes avec des fêtes.'* Charles was posted elsewhere and later sacked for malversation of stores accounts.

A portrait of Josephine Bonaparte by Isabey.

These preoccupations did not impair Napoleon's political and military competence. The republican ideologists wanted to bring the gospel of reason and equality to the whole world, as Trotsky did the determinism of Marx: but Napoleon was no ideologue; he was a Machiavellian realist who knew his Italians. He ordered his army to respect the Church, so powerful and rich, though he blackmailed it for money; and he played down the anti-Christian dogmas of the Revolution, for he always considered religion essential for social order and judged Christians and Muslims accordingly. Nor did he, on republican principles, topple the Piedmontese monarch: it was wiser to buy his neutrality.

For all their success in Lombardy, the position of the French was precarious. So, counting on a massive Austrian counter-attack over the Brenner, Napoleon gave the Austrians no respite, though he failed to evict them from Mantua. Through the rich Lombard country, with its tiled farmsteads, olive groves, rice fields and poplars, he advanced on Parma and Ferrara and the borders of Emilia Romagna to Bologna, the strategic key to the passes of the Apennines. The French soon occupied Florence, threatened Rome and even Naples, and were bought off. But his

OPPOSITE Dabos's painting of Napoleon as First Consul. As impressive as his military feats were his achievements and innovations as an administrator.

main concern was to contain the avalanche of an Austrian counter-stroke over the mountains. That autumn, as the vineyards ripened to the vintage, the country between Lake Garda and Mantua became the strategic prize. Peschiera, where the Mincio flows into Garda; Verona on the Adige, commanding the passes of the Alps; Legnano down river, and Mantua with its elaborate defences, formed the 'quadrilateral' recurrent in Italian military history.

In late July 1796 came the first attack, as a new Austrian army under the Alsatian General Wurmser made a three-pronged advance: south-west down the Val di Soli on Brescia and Napoleon's life-line to Milan; down both sides of Garda, aiming at the French besieging Mantua; and south-east by Rovereto on Verona. The gravest threat was to Brescia, so Napoleon at once concentrated

Napoleon aiming the cannon at the battle of Lodi in May 1796.

to destroy it and caught the Austrians at Castiglione south of Desenzano on Garda. He then struck north up the Adige along the Val Largarina east of the lake, routed the Austrians at Rovereto and took Trento, the main hub of Austrian communication with Bolzano and the Brenner. He then turned south down the Val Sugana, defeated the second attack by Alvinzi at Bassano and made him fall back towards Mantua. Failing to take Verona, Napoleon then wheeled to attack the communications with Mantua, crossing the Adige from the east. Seizing a standard, he himself led the rush on the bridge at Arcola, was thrust off it and only rescued by Lucien Bonaparte and Marmont, afterwards a marshal. The attack just came off. Then, in 1797, a fresh Austrian army from the north was defeated in the Val Largarina at Rivoli, and this victory was final. Wurmser, shut up in Mantua, had to

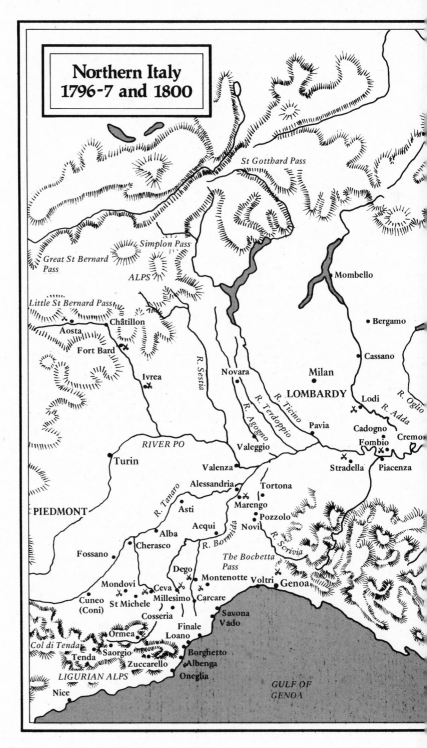

Northern Italy
1796-7 and 1800

St Gotthard Pass

Simplon Pass

Great St Bernard
Pass

ALPS

Mombello

Little St Bernard Pass

Châtillon

Aosta

Bergamo

Fort Bard

Cassano

Ivrea

R. Sestia

Novara

Milan

LOMBARDY

Lodi

R. Oglio

R. Ticino

R. Terdoppio

Pavia

Cadogno

R. Adda

R. Agogno

Fombio

Cremo

RIVER PO

Valeggio

Turin

Valenza

Stradella

Piacenza

PIEDMONT

R. Tanaro

Alessandria

Tortona

Asti

Marengo

Acqui

Pozzolo

Alba

Novil

R. Scrivia

Cherasco

R. Bormida

Fossano

The Bochetta
Pass

Dego

Mondovi

Ceva

Montenotte

Voltri

Genoa

Cuneo
(Coni)

St Michele

Millesimo

Carcare

Cosseria

Savona

Finale

Vado

Ormea

Loano

Col di Tenda

Tenda

Saorgio

Borghetto

Zuccarello

Albenga

LIGURIAN ALPS

Oneglia

GULF OF
GENOA

Nice

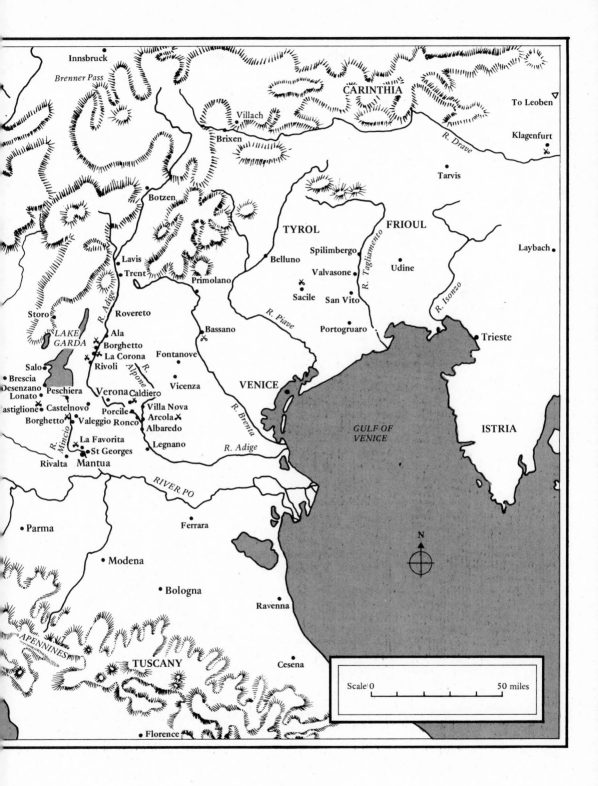

Innsbruck

Brenner Pass

CARINTHIA

To Leoben

Villach

R. Drave

Brixen

Klagenfurt

Tarvis

Botzen

TYROL

FRIOUL

Laybach

Lavis

Spilimbergo

Belluno

Valvasone

R. Tagliamento

Udine

Trent

Primolano

R. Piave

Sacile

San Vito

R. Isonzo

Storo

Rovereto

Bassano

Portogruaro

Trieste

*LAKE
GARDA*

Ala

Borghetto

La Corona

Fontanove

VENICE

Rivoli

R. Alpone

Salo

Vicenza

Brescia

Verona

Caldiero

*GULF OF
VENICE*

ISTRIA

Desenzano

Peschiera

Lonato

astiglione

Castelnovo

Porcile

Villa Nova

Borghetto

Valeggio

Ronco

Arcola

R. Brenta

Albaredo

La Favorita

Legnano

R. Adige

Rivalta

St Georges

Mantua

RIVER PO

Parma

Ferrara

Modena

Bologna

Ravenna

N

APENNINES

TUSCANY

Cesena

Scale 0   50 miles

Florence

surrender: 'They've sent a young madman', remarked an Austrian officer, speaking for many of his kind before and since, 'who attacks right, left and from the rear. It's an intolerable way of making war.' The whole campaign in the quadrilateral had taken less than six months.

But Napoleon was still wary: new Austrian armies were being concentrated and the synchronized French attack on the Rhine had failed. After the depredations of the French, Italy was seething with resentment and the Directory in Paris was even more insecure. He had to bring back peace as well as victory, if on his own terms. So, advancing on Vienna by the easy route through Udine, Villach and Klagenfurt, he halted a hundred miles from the city and, in April 1797, on his own authority, concluded a preliminary peace at Leoben in the Steirmark which preserved the French conquests in Italy. 'Haven't we killed enough men', he wrote for the record to the Austrian Archduke Charles, 'and done enough damage to suffering humanity?'

That summer Napoleon held court at the Villa Cerutti, a *palazzo* outside Milan at Mombello, and Josephine and the *de facto* ruler of Italy took their ease on Maggiore. The Cispadane Republic, set up the previous October, was now incorporated in a Cisalpine Republic which included some Venetian territory. A Ligurian Republic was created at Genoa: the French had already occupied Ancona, and Napoleon had concluded the Peace of Tolentino with the Pope, who paid a large indemnity and ceded the strategically important city of Bologna. The constitutions of these artificial republics favoured the upper bourgeoisie, and there was much eloquence about a free and resurgent Italy: but Napoleon, himself basically Italian, had no illusions.

Meanwhile, at Mombello, the political general remained alert. Predictably, there was now another crisis in Paris, where the Directory had to put down the communist conspiracy of Babeuf, while the political general Pichegru, who had conquered Holland and was now President of the Assembly, was trying to restore the Bourbons. The English, following the defection of Spain, rebellion in Ireland and mutinies in the fleet, now seemed readier to come to terms; but in spite of his message to the Archduke Charles, Napoleon was interested only in his own kind of peace. 'Do you believe that I triumph in Italy for the Carnots, Barras, etc.?'; once the war was over, he would have to 'pay court to the barristers of the Luxembourg'. 'Peace may be necessary to satisfy these Paris ninnies, and if it has to be made, it is for me to make it.'

As in the late Roman Empire, the rival political generals were manœuvring at the centre of power. Another general, Hoche, in command of the Army of Sambre et Meuse, moved up towards Paris on the pretext of concentrating for an expedition against Ireland; he was ordered back to base, where, conveniently for Napoleon, he died. Napoleon was more subtle: he would for the present preserve the Republic, but he would make it dependent on himself. So he sent the ex-Jacobin Augereau, one of his toughest generals, to Paris; and on 4 September 1797 (18 *Fructidor*), in collaboration with the Republican Directors, the General surrounded the Tuileries, arrested or dispersed the royalist leaders and saved the Republic. It now relied on Napoleon's bayonets.

He soon concluded the long negotiations following the preliminary peace at Leoben by the Peace of Campo Formio, signed at Udine in October 1797, which shared out northern Italy with Austria. In return for Lombardy and for recognizing the Cisalpine Republic, which now embraced Modena, Ferrara, Bologna and parts of Emilia Romagna, the Austrians obtained Venice, all her territories up to the Adige, and Istria and Dalmatia into the bargain. Napoleon thus extinguished the most ancient, august and picturesquely decadent republic in Europe; a brutal exercise in power politics, only partially offset when, under Austrian influence, Venetian cooking became the best in Italy.

And Venice led Napoleon's thoughts to the Levant. France obtained the Venetian sphere of influence in Albania, for what that was worth; in the Ionian Isles Corfu, St Maura (Levkas) and Zante as well as Ithaca, commanding the entrance to the Adriatic and the Gulf of Corinth: France, not Venice, might dominate the Levant. It was a triumphant settlement, though flawed by two considerations: Austria still retained a strategic foothold in Italy, and the Austrian Netherlands had also been ceded to the French. So long as they retained them and remained set on further expansion, Great Britain might well continue the war; if necessary for years, but not, in view of the colossal British wealth created by the Industrial Revolution, necessarily alone.

In Napoleon's eighteenth-century mind, the days of the Revolution were now numbered: 'What an idea,' he remarked at Mombello – 'a republic of thirty million with our morals and our vices!' But he was still, on the face of it, its servant and he was a master of political timing.

The Directory was in no hurry to see him in Paris, so they

appointed him to represent France at the Congress of Rastadt, where he again won too many laurels – securing Salzburg and Breisgau for France. He returned to Paris in December 1797, with so little intention of hanging about that within six months he would leave for Egypt; meanwhile, he played his political hand coolly, and the conqueror of Italy became the architect of peace. He got himself elected to the *Institut de France* and wore its civilian uniform on formal occasions; he held aloof from the febrile and dangerous intrigues of the Directory: he bided his time. 'The Gallic temperament', he wrote, 'is ill accustomed to that great calculation of time: yet it is solely in virtue of this that I have succeeded in everything that I have done.'

But he had to keep in the public eye. 'In Paris', he said, 'nothing is remembered for long. If I remain doing nothing long I am lost.' The Directory had now given him the command of the Army of England, and he inspected the rudimentary preparations at Calais and at Ostend, but the sight of the Channel and its eastern approaches in February was not encouraging, and obviously the French Navy could not dominate the Straits: 'Too chancy', remarked Napoleon, 'to risk *la belle France* on the throw of a dice.'

But there was another way to strike at England: already, in the previous August, Napoleon had written to the Directors from Italy, 'The day is not far off when we shall appreciate the necessity, in order really to destroy England, to seize Egypt.' In fact, the project was not original; well before the Revolution, the idea had been canvassed in official and business circles in Paris, notably by the Comte de Choiseul; and the traditional pro-Turkish policy as a make-weight against the Hapsburgs had already been questioned. Egypt might become a French colony; a project was already being discussed to cut a canal from Suez to the Mediterranean, and the failure of the French in India made them seek strategic and economic compensation nearer home. Thus the first eighteenth-century European 'colonialist' adventure in civilized Africa, as opposed to settlement at the Cape and slave-trading outposts on the west coast, was to be in Egypt, destined in 1956 to be the scene of the Suez Crisis – the last one.

Napoleon had already accepted the appointment to Constantinople, and the romantic side of his nature had long been fascinated by the East, where he would be more untrammelled even than in Italy – a ruler on his own. For their part, the Directory wanted more plunder and they wanted to get rid of the General.

So the rash and sensational project was sanctioned. Charles-

Talleyrand, sketched by
d'Orsay. He supported
Napoleon's Egyptian project,
but was later to dissociate
himself entirely from
the Emperor.

Maurice de Talleyrand-Périgord, that master of calculation, whom
the Revolution had translated from the minor bishopric of Autun
to become by 1797 Minister for Foreign Affairs, now proved the
most effective advocate of the expedition, and he would play a
decisive part in Napoleon's career. Lamed in childhood and so
passed over for a great inheritance, Talleyrand had been relegated
to the Church, but had become a celebrated wit, gambler and rake
during the *ancien régime*. Despairing of Louis XVI, he had joined
the Revolution, been sent as an envoy to London, fled to the
United States; but after Robespierre's fall he had returned to
France. Barras had soon seen his brilliance, and in fact this venal
and treacherous *bon viveur* would prove to be a statesman in the
tradition of Richelieu and Mazarin, with a cold view of essentials
and an imperturbable urbanity and finesse in public affairs. His
interest in colonial enterprise had led him to advocate Choiseul's

plan, though he was wary enough to pull out of it when it looked likely to fail. And now, like his masters, he hoped that the great powers would be diverted from attacking Revolutionary France by partitioning the Turkish Empire, and that French losses in the West Indies as well as India would be compensated in Egypt. Moreover, now that the French had levied thirty million francs from the bankers of Berne, there was something in the treasury and the chance was taken. The preparations took only ten weeks and they were so sketchy that the troops had to march across the desert without water bottles.

Napoleon never allowed pleasure seriously to interfere with war and he decided at first to leave Josephine behind. In May 1798, at Toulon, she tried hard to prove herself indispensable; and here General Dumas, the West Indian mulatto father of the novelist, came in useful to his Commander-in-Chief. 'She wants to go with me to Egypt,' said Bonaparte, 'Are you taking your wife along, Dumas?' 'No, by God', said this honest man, 'she'd be a great embarrassment to me.' Napoleon went to Egypt without his wife.

When, on 19 May 1798, the main expedition of more than thirty-five thousand troops, their transports escorted by thirteen battleships, got under way out of Toulon, Napoleon was taking a risky gamble. The British Mediterranean fleet, withdrawn two years earlier, had now been dispatched by Pitt to deal with any French initiative, whether out to the Atlantic or east to the Levant, and Nelson had been in the offing two days before; but a north wind that had brought the French east of Corsica was much fiercer west of it, and the British had to delay in Sardinia to repair their ships.

Napoleon, sincerely zealous for the civilizing mission of France, had included in the expedition a 'living encyclopaedia' of scientists, orientalists, zoologists, artists and writers, and a poet. Gaspard Monge, mathematician, engineer and expert in making guns, had been Minister of Marine and a main founder of the *École Polytechnique*; he had also organized the plunder of Italian works of art, so he knew the ropes in Rome and procured Arabic type from the papal Office of Propaganda. He was to prove Napoleon's most reliable expert. The zoologist Saint Hilaire, who had written the standard work on the orang-outang, would now write the standard work on the crocodile; the chemist Berthollet, the economist Say, the statistician Fourier (no relative of the political theorist), the orientalist Champollion who first deciphered the Egyptian hieroglyphs, were all on board. The poet was called François Auguste Parseval-Grandmaison; he had translated Camoen's *Lusiads*, but failed himself to stay the full course of adventure. These eminent men were naturally despised by the soldiery, who called them 'Pekinese' and 'Asses'; and Napoleon's discussions with them, which senior officers were expected to attend, were thought a great bore – as indeed such desultory discussions are apt to be.

Having narrowly missed being intercepted by Nelson with fourteen ships of the line off Sicily, by 10 June the French descended on Malta. Valetta was potentially impregnable behind the colossal fortifications that had once defied the full might of the Turks; but the knights had lost the habit of war, and the numerous French ones were politically divided. Some had joined the émigrés on the Rhine, and the estates of the Order in France had been confiscated; others had been won over by French diplomacy, and the new Grand Master, Ferdinand von Hompesch, had ill-advisedly accepted an offer of protection from Tsar Paul I. Obviously the strategic island would go either to the British or the French.

There was only token resistance by peasant levies in the stone-walled fields; most lasting on Gozo, where they were ignorant of the surrender. Napoleon packed off the Grand Master, amid the jeers of the populace, to Trieste, gave all knights under sixty four days' notice to leave and promulgated a rational republican constitution in an island dominated by baroque churches and bells. He had sixty Maltese boys from the leading families sent to Paris to be turned into Frenchmen, and he revolutionized the island's posts and administration.

Apart from the majestic past of Egypt in antiquity, its remarkable civilization in the days of the Fatimids and of Saladin, and during the early phase of Mamlūk rule under Baybars and Al Nasir, when the great mosque of Cairo had been built and the Mongols repelled, the country had long fallen into decline. Its often brilliant Muslim culture had been socially superficial, based on the ruthless exploitation of the *fellahin*, and by the fifteenth century the Mamlūk rulers had become illiterate, drunken and even mad. One had two of his doctors beheaded for failing to cure him; another blinded an alchemist who had failed to turn base metal into gold. In 1517 the last Mamlūk Sultan had been hanged by the Ottoman Turks at the gates of Cairo, and Egypt had become a tributary backwater of the vast empire of the Grand Turk. But the Mamlūks, under the nominal suzerainty of Turkish

The strong fortifications at Valetta. The capture of Malta was made easy by the internal divisions among the Knights of St John.

viceroys, had continued to batten on the country. After a last flare-up when the Turks were fighting Russia, Ali Bey had over-run Palestine and even Mecca; but his death in 1773 had set off the usual struggle for the succession, and this revolt the French now made an excuse for invading Egypt, supposedly on behalf of the Sultan at Constantinople.

They found themselves in a very alien and run-down civiliza-tion – strangely silent and apathetic. When captured by the Bedouin and 'abundantly raped by their scrawny but vigorous captors', the young Frenchmen were badly shocked, though Napoleon merely told them that it was their own fault for getting taken. The Egyptians, for their part, were astonished at the sexual single-mindedness of the French.

On 30 June the expedition sighted Egypt, and at once Napoleon

wrote to the Directory, 'I hurled myself ashore', in spite of a choppy sea, on Marabut beach east of Alexandria. Alexandria was soon occupied and he struck inland. Ill-equipped for a desert trek, eighteen thousand men marched on Cairo and as the hot *Khamsin* wind set in, some went mad with thirst or shot themselves; there was bitter disillusionment and complaint. Afterwards Napoleon would order 'Please have measured in the presence of a staff officer how much water a camel carries in an ordinary goat skin' (answer: twenty-four gallons).

But the General, who would spend his soldiers' lives like depreciated currency, now had to strike before the annual flooding of the Nile and restore morale by victorious battle. At Shubra Kit, near Ramaniya on the western branch of the river, they first encountered the Mamlūks under the ferociously-bearded Murad

61

Napoleon in Egypt

Napoleon's campaign in Egypt had as its prime motive the thwarting of British power in India and it was the first French venture into the African arena. Militarily it was not a success but there were cultural achievements instead: the Rosetta stone was discovered and its hieroglyphs interpreted, and the architectural splendours along the Nile studied in mathematical detail.

FAR LEFT Gaspard Monge, the mathematician and engineer who accompanied the expedition.

LEFT Vivant Denon, the artist who recorded his impressions of Egypt.

BELOW LEFT A painting by Géricault of an incident during the Egyptian campaign.

BELOW Murad Bey, the Mamlūk leader whom Napoleon pursued down the Nile.

Bey. These picturesque warriors were mainly recruited from carefully-selected boys of twelve from the Caucasus, for whom the bed of their master was often the way to promotion. They formed a spirited elite, armed to the teeth and dressed up to the nines. On superb Arab horses they would charge home like wild-cats; then, if repulsed, vanish at speed: they carried much of their wealth on them in gold and rich apparel, and their appearance was medieval, elegant and colourful. Before eighteenth-century fire-power, they were an anachronism.

So the first brush set a familiar pattern of colonial warfare. The French formed squares: the Mamlūks, like the Seljuqs confronted with Crusaders, dashed around them, seeking a weak spot; then, when their Greek-crewed gunboats attacked the French flotilla, they charged. They were driven off by grapeshot and musketry, and when the Mamlūk flagship blew up, they made off. It had been an inconclusive encounter.

The French, with deteriorating discipline and morale, now trudged across the Libyan desert on Cairo. On 21 July, in blazing heat, at Embaba within sight of the pyramids of Gizeh, where, Napoleon told his entourage (not his army, already deployed for battle) that 'forty centuries looked down upon them', the main Mamlūk army was destroyed. They charged with their usual abandon, but the French held their fire, then shot them up and the artillery completed the rout. Murad Bey, with the remnant of his expensive cavalry, pulled out and disappeared in a cloud of dust towards Gizeh and Upper Egypt, while the Albanian infantry were shot to pieces and the *fellahin* clubmen dispersed. Those Mamlūks who, although encumbered with their finery, had taken to water were pole-axed or shot. The plunder was immense; in gold, in rich fabrics, in elaborate weapons.

Famous as it became, the battle of the Pyramids had not been, by Napoleon's later standards, at all large. The French claimed to have killed two thousand Mamlūks and put their own losses at most as twenty-nine dead and 120 wounded. It was all over in a couple of hours.

There was now panic in Cairo, and Napoleon moved down to Gizeh to the luxury of Murad Bey's own residence. The key towns of Egypt were his – Alexandria, Rosetta, Cairo. But when the French, in the blaze of summer, moved into the capital, they found, apart from the public splendour of mosques and palaces, a city of terrible heat, squalor, dust and flies; of beggars and disease and famished dogs; of mosquitoes and stench.

Undaunted, Napoleon at once set about creating the base of a permanent colony; then, scintillating with glory, he meant to return to France and make himself its master. He did not know that on 1 August 1798, nine days after the battle of the Pyramids, Nelson had destroyed the French fleet in Abuqīr Bay, in what became inaccurately celebrated as the battle of the Nile.

This brilliant feat of calculated daring and seamanship changed the strategic picture in the Mediterranean and beyond. The long arm of sea-power had got its first stranglehold on the 'land animal'. More decisive even than Trafalgar, the battle asserted British supremacy at sea. Hence the long blockade of Napoleon's over-extended Empire, which would lead to the wars in Spain and Russia and the final collapse. Immediately, it meant that the Turks, to whom Talleyrand had now been careful not to go as ambassador, declared war, and the following year saw the Second Coalition of Great Britain, Austria, Prussia, Naples and Turkey against France.

In Cairo, Napoleon put a good face on the disaster, but he had quite miscalculated: he had indeed insisted that Brueys enter Alexandria harbour or make for Corfu; but both instructions were too late, and should not have had to be re-iterated.

Napoleon now pretended that a colony was still viable. Here, as the Great Sultan – the *Sultan Kebir* – he was even more independent than in Italy, and he would look back upon the disastrous adventure as the most 'ideal time in his life' – that is, as the time when he had fullest scope to mould a civilization. His posture as a Muslim naturally failed to impress the conservative Egyptians, who detested all infidel Franks with a steady, impassive, if covert, hatred, and that October a rising took place in Cairo. 'Only the greatest severity', he had to report to the Directory, 'will make the Turks behave. Every day I have to have five or six heads cut off in the streets.' Fine projects for education and medicine came to nothing; but Egypt was properly mapped, and the work went forward for the famous volumes of the *Déscription d'Egypte* which first revealed ancient Egypt to the world and to the Egyptians. Next year the Rosetta stone was discovered, from which Champollion would decipher the hieroglyphs.

In pursuit of Murad Bey, an expedition now went up the Nile to Assiut, Thebes, Luxor and beyond: it included the artist Vivant Denon, and the Valley of the Kings, the Sphinx avenues, the gigantic temples, were viewed and recorded. Though the precarious regime was nearly bankrupt, the experts were happy.

ABOVE Napoleon's luxurious bathroom at Château
Rambouillet, from which he often attended to
affairs of state.

OPPOSITE Napoleon's bedroom at the Grand Trianon,
Versailles: a contrast to the more homely furnishings
of Malmaison.

Napoleon was less so. Incontrovertible evidence had arrived that Josephine was again flaunting her affair with Charles, and engaged in his dubious financial speculations, so that her husband was the laughing-stock of Paris. *'Il est cocu'* ('He is cuckolded'), they said. So the General, who wrote, 'the veil has at last fallen from my eyes', took a mistress – a pretty, plump blonde with blue eyes from Carcassonne. Her father unknown and her mother a cook, Pauline Fourès had followed the classic occupation of a little French milliner; then, nattily dressed as a Hussar, had accompanied her husband, Lieutenant Fourès, to Egypt. After Napoleon had pounced, she became 'Cléopatre' or *'L'Egyptienne du Général'* (*Anglice*, 'General's Egyptian, Sir'). King David had dispatched Uriah the Hittite to the front line, but Napoleon consigned Lieutenant Fourès to France. Intercepted by the British, he was humourously returned to Egypt on parole, whereupon Pauline divorced him. The liaison became official, and a new Cleopatra accompanied a new ruler of Egypt, to be abandoned, though afterwards provided for in France, when Napoleon left for Syria – as Palestine was then termed.

For Napoleon had resolved to defeat the Turks before they could attack Egypt; perhaps he even meant to press on to Constantinople; and leaving his administration and experts to run the potential colony, he launched a disastrous expedition against Gaza, Jaffa – where three thousand Turkish prisoners were shot out of hand – and Akko (Acre). Though he routed a large Turkish army under the northern slopes of Mount Tabor, at Akko he was repulsed: the British had prevented his siege guns coming by sea, and, commanded by the dashing Sir Sidney Smith, had reinforced the garrison. After a desperate struggle, all assaults failed and Smith won a romantic reputation, though he would later describe the affair so often and at such length that he became known as 'Long Acre'. Plague and dysentery had now broken out and though the General had shown cold courage in visiting and touching the sick in the filthy hospitals, the French had to make a gruelling retreat to Egypt. They had lost about six thousand men and the spoiling attack on the Turks had failed. Though, back in Egypt in July 1799, Napoleon routed a sea-borne Turkish army on the beaches of Abuqīr, it was plain that the Egyptian adventure was a fiasco.

So, characteristically, Napoleon cut his loss, the more impelled by the news thoughtfully provided by the British that the Russians were driving the French from Italy, and that the

Austrians were defeating them on the Danube. It was urgent at once to become the saviour of the Republic.

On the evening of 17 August, Napoleon left Cairo, giving out that he was going to Upper Egypt, and five days later he reached the outskirts of Alexandria. His entourage included Berthier and Murat, Monge and Denon, and the Mamlūk Roustam Raza, a young Armenian presented to him by a Cairene sheik, who would become Napoleon's valet and body-guard until his abdication. Unobtrusively, they went aboard the fast and heavily-armed frigate *La Muiron* which, together with *La Carrère*, reached France in just under seven weeks. Again Napoleon's luck had held: General Kléber, an Alsatian ex-architect, who succeeded him in command, had been diverted to Rosetta for an appointment that Napoleon had never meant to keep: he was furious, and his expletives represented the feelings of the troops. He inaugurated a tougher regime, following Napoleon's instructions to the military governor of Cairo to 'chop off six heads a day and keep smiling'. But Kléber would be assassinated by an Egyptian in the following year.

Napoleon had been blamed for thus ratting on his expedition: but he had taken the only realistic course: any self-respecting rat would have done it. Though he had in fact been written off by the Directory, his only chance was now to return to the centre of power; as Markham well puts it, 'The moment was at hand which would bring him to supreme power or the guillotine.'

4 First Consul 1799-1804

Liberty is the need of a small class privileged with higher ability than the rest of mankind. Equality, on the other hand, pleases the masses.

NAPOLEON

THE FRANCE TO WHICH NAPOLEON RETURNED was becoming increasingly hard to govern. As Professor Cobb has shown, the whole society had been profoundly shaken up. 'There is no doubt', he writes, 'that the Revolution by greatly adding to the picturesque elements in eighteenth century life, and by enormously extending both the range and depth of mobility . . . extended the range of opportunity and enterprise. . . . In the general spectacle of carnage, violence, vengeance and intransigence, one would at least like to think so.' It had also 'enormously extended the hate category'. The atrocities committed by the *Sans Culottes* were equalled by those of the terrorists of the Counter-Revolution – *'Je t'ouvrirai les tripes'*, 'I'll open your guts for you', said one woman. Further 'The Revolution in its later stages was a particularly arduous time for all those, especially the aged and infirm, who suffered from the cold.' Drunkenness had become 'a source of popular violence and ferocity . . . and there is plenty of evidence that the *massacreurs* of September 1792 had been wildly drunk throughout the horrible proceedings'. 'DeChristianization', the abolition of Sundays and the ridiculous Republican calendar calling 1792 the year I, had infuriated the Catholic majority, particularly the women; families had been disrupted, children giving evidence against parents, brother against brother. Everywhere opportunity beckoned for blackguards and crooks. The Thermidorian reaction of July 1794 had tried to put the upper bourgeoisie back in the saddle, but a roar of vitriolic protest went on: 'It took a Robespierre to induce the French – temporarily – to watch what they said', and he had not lasted. The virulent hatreds surpassed anything in the English Civil Wars, and France is still marked by the trauma.

Recurrent dearth and even famine were aggravated by the economic 'imperialism of Paris', by requisitioning and by dislocation of markets and transport, by brigandage in the country and violence in the towns. Hence increased bitterness between the peasants and the urban revolutionaries, further exacerbated by the contrast between the ostentation and gourmandizing of the parvenu rulers and the misery of the poor, who 'disputed scraps of stale bread with dogs'. Bread riots were frequent, the 'problem of subsistence' acute.

Napoleon was determined to bring order into this chaos, to get society back to normal without reviving the *ancien régime*, and he knew that he could count on a great body of middling opinion, the real Third Estate, independent of the extremists in

PREVIOUS PAGES Napoleon faces the abuse of the Council of Five Hundred: an engraving by Geoffroy.

72

either camp. But first, he was convinced, the constitution must be scrapped: the Directorate of August 1795 as consolidated by Napoleon's 'whiff of grapeshot' and Augereau's *coup* in *Fructidor* 1797, was in theory elected by the Council of *Anciens* and dependent on the Assembly of Five Hundred; in fact, to obtain any stability, elections had to be rigged and deputies 'purged'. Executive and legislature were chronically at odds. Meanwhile, a raging inflation had developed in the *assignat* paper money, and since a return of the Bourbons seemed on the cards, government bonds secured on the lands of the *émigrés* and the Church commanded little confidence. The plunder of Italy and Berne had tided over a crisis, but Egypt had brought in nothing, and the government was head over ears in debt, the troops unpaid; while the conquests in Italy had now been lost, and the position on the Rhine only just redeemed by Masséna, the ex-smuggler and ranker, who had won his reputation in Italy. 'What have you done', Napoleon could well say, 'with the France I left so glorious?'

Two possibilities seemed imminent – a return to a regime of Left Wing terror, led by the political General Bernadotte, Minister

A contemporary engraving depicts starving crowds queuing for bread outside a baker's in the winter of 1794.

for War, or a counter-revolution, for which Barras was intriguing, to restore the Bourbons. Somebody was going to make a *coup d'état*: Napoleon was determined that it would be himself.

Nor in the event did he miscalculate. There was a massive interest among many politicians, the *haute bourgeoisie* and the small property-owners in town and country in stabilizing a settlement. They would even prove ready for a new dynasty to keep the old one out – to protect their property and even their lives. It was this great interest of the solid core of France that the Consulate would represent. And Talleyrand (who 'during those years laid the foundations of a tremendous fortune' as well as probably siring the painter Delacroix and taking up with a Mrs Grand, formerly the mistress of Sir Philip Francis in India) had decided that Napoleon was his man.

Napoleon's immediate position was domestically difficult and politically dangerous. Josephine, who had rushed to meet him but taken the wrong road, had dissuaded him from divorcing her by weeping all night outside his locked door, then sending Eugène and her daughter Hortense to mediate. A divorce would then have been politically deleterious and Josephine had useful contacts to lull the Directors whom Napoleon intended to expel. One of them, who found Madame Bonaparte attractive, would be asked to luncheon for the day planned for Napoleon's *coup*.

Meanwhile Bernadotte, who, when King of Sweden, was to turn on Napoleon, moved that he be outlawed for his unauthorized return; but the Directors, unwilling to face the rage of the populace who already regarded the General as a saviour, turned the proposal down. The moderates were soon sounding him out. The ex-Abbé, the Director Sieyès, a veteran of the original Revolution and an expert on constitutions, and Talleyrand, the most cunning realist of them all, now planned to change the whole unpractical set-up of *Les Anciens* and the Five Hundred. Sieyès even hoped to make Napoleon his instrument, projecting a provisional government of three 'Consuls' as in Berne, but with much greater executive powers. He might have known that Napoleon would take and keep the lion's share. The conspirators now won over Fouché – another ex-Abbé and Minister of Police; then General Lefebvre, the Military Governor of Paris and a former sergeant major, who, once he had taken in the idea, proved eager 'to throw those b----s of lawyers' into the Seine. But the *coup* proved a bungled affair, only just carried through with the thinnest veneer of legality.

General Bernadotte, who later became Charles XIV of Sweden. Napoleon called him 'an intriguer whom I cannot trust'.

The first problem was to persuade the *Anciens* and the Five Hundred to supersede themselves, and to get them, under military protection, where the conspirators wanted them. Convened at the chilling hour of 5 a.m. on 18 *Brumaire* (9 November), the *Anciens* voted that both Councils should meet at St Cloud outside Paris, and appointed Napoleon to the command of the Paris garrison; a draft decree that he promptly altered to include that of the Directorial Guard. Barras had been bought off by Talleyrand for half a million francs, and the other two Directors had been detained in the Luxembourg.

By mid-day, Napoleon arrived at St Cloud, where the meeting of the Councils had been delayed while the place was got ready, and he found both in recalcitrant mood. Told that the Directors

Lucien Bonaparte, brother of
Napoleon: he saved the
situation at St Cloud.

had resigned, the *Anciens* were voting to elect new ones; so the
General decided to confront them. But with civilians he lost his
sure touch: for about the first time in his career, he appeared
embarrassed, spoke incoherently and tried to bully them: 'The
God of War and the God of luck are marching with me!' *'Mon
Général'*, interposed his secretary Bourienne, 'get out of here, you
don't know what you're saying.' So Napoleon tried his luck with
the Five Hundred, many of them Jacobins, who were debating in
the *Orangerie* of the château. He found himself in a bear-garden
and himself the bear: arriving with a few Directorial Guards, he
was greeted with *'Hors la loi! A bas le Tyran!'* ('Outlaw! Down
with the tyrant!'); Lucien, though President, could not control
the enraged deputies, who manhandled Napoleon and scratched
his face, unless in a Corsican passion, he did it himself. He was

rescued by the Guards, though his disarray roused their natural instinct to turn on failure.

But all was not lost. Lucien kept his head, got through a message that the session must be closed at once and gave Napoleon ten minutes. So a captain and ten Directorial Guards escorted the President out of the *Orangerie*, and, legally speaking, the Council of Five Hundred had ceased to exist. Then Sieyès, the civilian, suggested that the Guards should be sent in, and Lucien and Napoleon lied to them. 'As President of the Five Hundred', shouted Lucien, 'I declare to you that the Council is being terrorized by a few deputies armed with *stilettos*' (an Italianate touch) – 'brigands', doubtless, 'in English pay'. Napoleon followed him up, a just man outraged: 'I wished to speak to them: they answered me with daggers!' So failure was cleverly exploited. Headed by Murat and to a roll of drums, a column of Guards with fixed bayonets went in; the ordinary garrison troops had not been used, but the deputies climbed or tumbled through the big windows of the *Orangerie* into the autumn dusk.

That evening, the *Anciens* nominated the three Consuls, Sieyès, Ducos and Napoleon; and Lucien, back in Paris, assembled a rump of deputies to clinch the decision. It was put out that an attempt to assassinate the General had been foiled. The Parisians acclaimed the *fait accompli*, with its bogus constitutional face; they wanted no more *coups d'état*.

The external situation which confronted the precarious Consulate was grave. In the spring of 1799 the Russians, infuriated by the French capture of Malta, of which the Tsar Paul had made himself Grand Prior of the Knights, had joined the Second Coalition. In alliance with the Austrians, who had defeated the French on the Danube, they had descended on Italy by the Gotthard in winter, and overwhelmed the French at Novi, while the creation of a Republic in Rome and a Parthenopean Republic in Naples had already landed the French in more trouble. The English, meanwhile, in concert with the Russians, had landed in Holland. This ill-found expedition under the Duke of York was soon driven out, Masséna defeated the Russians at Zurich and the worst had been staved off; but France was still in danger, an added reason for strong government.

This Sieyès's academic plans for a regime of checks and balances, with Napoleon as ornamental Grand Elector, could not provide. So Napoleon forced through a Constitution which gave

OVERLEAF The Treaty of Leoben signed in Italy on 17 April 1797, painted by Lethière. This preliminary peace set the seal on the French conquests in Italy.

Emanuel Joseph, Count
Sieyès, one of the three
Consuls and President of
the Senate.

the three Consuls a decade of office and that extendable, with a First Consul entirely predominant. Sieyès was pacified by being made President of the Senate and compromised by the gift of a 'national' estate. The other Consuls were merely advisory. Cambacérès was a gourmet of deviant tastes, who remarked, when guests talked too much over the *foie gras*, 'Hush, we can't concentrate'; Lebrun was an economist who had served the old regime, happily concerned with the mysteries of his calling. Talleyrand called them *'Hic, haec, hoc'*, best translated 'he, she and it'. By 14 December the Consulate, endorsed by a plebiscite in February 1800, which gave three million Frenchmen in its favour, if four million abstained, was in being. 'The powers of the state must be strong and stable', said the Consuls' manifesto, 'the revolution takes its stand upon the principles with which it began. It is now finished.'

When, in February, the first Consul and his colleagues moved into their official residence, Napoleon remarked 'It isn't everything to be in the Tuileries. The thing is to stay there.' More subtle, when someone observed that the grand rooms were gloomy, he observed, 'Yes, and so is glory!' He was still only thirty years old.

The Consular regime was a dictatorship, but as much civilian as military.

For the first time since 1789, the Constitution contained no declaration or guarantee of the Rights of Man, no mention of liberty, equality or fraternity. . . . Bonaparte alone, as first Consul, was invested with vast legislative and executive powers. He alone could initiate laws and nominate ministers, generals, civil servants, magistrates and members of the Council of State.

The co-opted eighty Senators were nominated for life; the legislative body proved a rubber stamp, and the Tribunal was supposed to consider, but not to initiate, legislation. Universal suffrage was rendered innocuous since only chosen 'notables' could be voted for, and the referendum was meant merely to endorse government power.

It was now possible to get down to business and to create institutions, laws and administration which lastingly transformed France and some of the countries that Napoleon was to incorporate in his brief Empire. But before reconstructing France, Napoleon had to defeat her enemies, and in the inevitable campaign of 1800 he lost no time. Already in January he ordered big troop concentrations round Dijon in Burgundy which could reinforce the

Armies of the Rhine and of Italy. For he had conceived a brilliant and hazardous strategy: while the Rhine army attacked, the main stroke would come in Italy, where the Austrians, who had driven the French back on Genoa, were now overextended. He proposed to supply his base at Villeneuve at the end of the Lake of Geneva from Geneva and Lausanne, then cross the Alps from Martigny across the high St Bernard passes down to Aosta, and so, with thirty thousand men, by Châtillon down the Dora Ballea valley to Ivrea, and so to threaten Turin and all the Austrian bases in Lombardy.

By mid-May, in spite of a hold-up at Bardo, the army under Berthier was in Aosta. Napoleon now crossed the St Bernard and rested for the night in the hospice: no great feat in early summer; arduous but not dangerous when done by mule and not, as David painted him, on a prancing horse. The Official Bulletin made the most of the feat, describing how the First Consul had slid over the snow and leaped precipices: in fact, only the guns had presented a major problem and been put on sledges improvised with tree trunks. By 2 June he was in Milan. 'We have come down like a thunderbolt', wrote Napoleon, 'the enemy was not expecting us at all and can hardly believe it.'

Then, on 14 June, came the climax. The Austrians, who had now taken Genoa and did not realize that the French were in force, advanced north from Alessandria across the Bormida and confronted Napoleon at Marengo with far more men and guns, for he had tried to outflank them by detaching two divisions. Their General Mélas had more initiative than most Austrian commanders, and Napoleon's strategic success had been tactically jeopardized. It was not until the French had nearly been overwhelmed that Desaix's division rejoined the main army, then in a swift counter-attack in which Desaix was shot dead, routed the enemy. The following day the Austrians signed an armistice and retired on Mantua.

Marengo was one of the narrowest of Napoleon's victories. It was politically crucial, for Paris was seething with conspiracies to replace him. In terms of human well-being, it also became memorable when the First Consul's chef created *poulet Marengo* out of the local olive oil, mushrooms, tomato and *vino bianco* – though without the garlic which, oddly enough, Napoleon disliked.

The first Consul at once returned to Paris. Here, even his brother

Jean-Jacques Regis de Cambacérès, the gourmet second Consul.

OVERLEAF The battle of Marengo. Despite a temporary reverse, victory was Napoleon's on 14 June 1800.

Joseph had been conspiring to replace him, Talleyrand had been reinsuring himself, and the other Consuls, Cambacérès and Lebrun, were cyphers. Rival generals were already in the wings, jostling for the succession and capable of fighting over it. Having ended the Revolution, Napoleon had to end the war.

Within less than two years he did so, though not for long. The Austrian Court had conceded only local defeat and with *Kaiserlich und Königlich* arrogance, had repudiated the armistice, so the First Consul had to stay in Paris. Fortunately in December Moreau defeated the Austrians at Höhenlinden on the Danube, and by February 1801 the Treaty of Lunéville restored all the French gains of Campo Formio and added to them. In September 1800 the British had seized Malta and so infuriated the Tsar Paul, who left the disintegrating Second Coalition and organized a League of Armed Neutrality of the Baltic powers against them. The British Navy thereupon, in the cold of January 1801, smashed the Danish fleet at Copenhagen – neutral or not: the occasion when in jest – for he had secretly been given the option to decide – Nelson put his telescope to his blind eye and finished the job. In March the Tsar Paul was strangled in his bedroom with an officer's scarf during a Palace revolution, when 'resisting' a demand to abdicate, and was succeeded by his son, now the guilt-ridden Tsar Alexander I.

The British were forced to a compromise, even though the French still dominated Belgium and the Batavian Republic, as well as an Helvetian one in Switzerland and Cispadine and Ligurian republics in Italy. In March 1801 Pitt had resigned after the King had refused Catholic emancipation in Ireland and after the French had capitulated in Egypt; in March 1802 Addington could make the Peace of Amiens. England retained Ceylon, but not even Martinique, only Trinidad.

As the threat of the Second Coalition receded and France emerged with her main conquests restored, Napoleon had been organizing the country to consolidate his regime. At first all was precarious. He had to keep an eye on the generals – under the Empire he would load them with honours and wealth to give them an interest in the settlement and to keep them out of politics. He had to pack Lucien off as Ambassador to Madrid for circulating a pamphlet, *Caesar, Cromwell and Bonaparte*, demanding who his heir could be. All now hung on Napoleon's life: in October 1800 the Jacobins tried to assassinate him at the Opera, and on Christmas Eve the royalists very nearly got him with a large bomb concealed

The assassination attempt on Napoleon in the Rue Niçaise, instigated by Georges Cadoudal: a cartoonist's impression.

in a wine cask in a cart slewed across the Rue Niçaise. It missed him only because his coachman, rather drunk to celebrate the season, drove at speed past the obstacle, so that the explosion only wrecked some houses and killed nine people. This *attentat*, planned by Breton royalists, led to a round-up of extremists of both camps. Josephine, in the next carriage, was badly shaken, but Napoleon's success and the common dangers of precarious grandeur had reconciled Napoleon and his wife; and her position, she hoped, was consolidated when Hortense was married to Louis Bonaparte, in spite of the hostility of the Bonaparte clan.

Napoleon's versatile genius, his fierce industry and will, his

Machiavellian diplomatic flair, now had full scope in the most creative phase of his career. First he had to secure his position. Early in 1800 he had suppressed most of the highly articulate Parisian political journals: 'If the press were not bridled', he said, 'I would not remain three days in power.' He had also tightened up his control of the army and the police. Under the Directory, conscription had been imposed on all men between twenty-one and twenty-five, though the better-off could buy themselves out of it; Napoleon now developed the military side of the *École Polytechnique* and founded the *École Special de St Cyr* to provide more officers. His regime would gradually become more authoritarian, cutting across the normal procedures of the law in the ponderous regime of the Empire.

So fortified, the First Consul turned to the reconstruction of France. He cannot have known much about it at first hand, but he soon learned. If his part in the transformation has been exaggerated, he gave it its impulse and he was a tiger for detail. He and his men tackled the administration, the finances, the law and the relationship of State and Church. The civil administration was already centralized, for the original Revolution had given the country uniform institutions – the Departments and Communes superseding the old regional and local divisions. The old Council of State was now restored and packed with Napoleon's nominees: later he would add young *auditeurs* who sat in on and assisted its proceedings, a nucleus of a professional civil service. Then the Departments were brought under closer control: all powers were transferred to *préfets* – another Roman touch – appointed by government, and they in turn nominated the *maires* of the *Communes*. The *préfets* came from outside and were well paid; the *maires* were unpaid and appointed from local men of substance. There was no nonsense about local elections: the revolutionary principle of local autonomy was reversed and all was now centralized. The judges, no longer elected, were now appointed by the government and irremovable. All the old professionals, the barristers, solicitors, clerks and ushers, reappeared, though a new *cour de cassation* was created – a central court of final appeal. Taxation, too, was centralized and *controlleurs*, collectors, treasurers, *vérificateurs* and registrars swelled the new bourgeois bureaucracy. A *Banque de France* was set up, mainly financed by the bankers behind the *coup d'état*. Education was made a centralized public service and centred on a *Universitaire de France*. In sum, 'Frenchmen ceased to be citizens and once more became subjects, no longer of a King but of a Government'; and 'This centralization ... has continued under varying political systems to provide the permanent structure of public life down to the present day.'

Within this lasting framework, Napoleon now initiated a Benthamite rationalization of the law. The *Code Civil*, later known as the *Code Napoléon*, finally superseded a welter of regional and local law and customs, feudal and Canon Law. It was a compromise between the Roman Law of the south and the customary, Teutonic, law of the north. It became the guarantee of the land settlement that stabilized the Revolution. As Napoleon intended, it strengthened the family; restored the authority of the father; subordinated women and children; reduced the occasions for divorce; reaffirmed traditional morality with a modern rationalistic sanction; and secured the rights of property and inheritance. All were still theoretically equal before the law, but in court, where evidence was taken, the employer was more equal than the employee. It was the charter of the bourgeoisie and of a *laissez faire* economy. This *Code Civil* was reinforced by a rationalization of the communal and penal codes, and in all these reforms Napoleon has at least the credit of making the lawyers work fast.

The Concordat with the Church of 1802 was a clever political stroke. The masses were still mainly Catholic, and it was urgent to rally the conservative forces of religion to government. Napoleon, the realist, had no use for the synthetic religions of the early *idéologues*; he preferred what has been termed 'good resolute nonsense backed by authority'. So when, in 1800, Pius VI died in exile in Valence, and Pius VII, who had already collaborated with the French, succeeded him, Napoleon did a deal in which naturally the First Consul had the advantage. After 'the restoration of the Altars', France was still a secular state and Catholicism was not the official religion, but it was recognized as that of the majority of Frenchmen. Nor, of course, were confiscated Church properties and tithes restored; the bishops and principal curés were paid, exiguously, by the state; the lesser clergy remained impoverished and dependent on their superiors. The proud, rich and aristocratic Church of the old regime had vanished.

In the contest over who should invest bishops, Napoleon also won. He now appointed the bishops, and the Pope consecrated them, while state control of public worship was revived. The recalcitrant clergy, and those who, while still in communion with

Rome, had taken the oath to the state, could now in time be reconciled with the new constitutional clergy; but in fact Napoleon, by uniting the Church in allegiance to the Pope, had created an Ultramontane when he had wanted a Gallican establishment.

This restoration of Christian morale, for Calvinists and Lutherans were also tolerated and established, was reinforced by more secular encouragements. No Corsican would have been unaware of the principle of 'jobs for the boys', and Napoleon packed the new institutions with applicants from all parties; even *émigrés* were encouraged to return and many did so. What was more, he played upon the national vanity by creating the Legion of Honour – at first mainly a military affair, but increasingly comprehending civilians. After all, Napoleon observed, 'It is by baubles that men are governed.'

The recognition of his work came quickly, before it was fully under way: in 1802 his tenure of office as First Consul was extended for life. So when, in March 1802, the Peace of Amiens had been signed with Great Britain, Napoleon was at a peak of popularity and success; as Markham puts it, 'the most dazzling embodiment of the enlightened despot in action'. He could now have settled for a balance of power and become accepted by the ruling classes of Europe; but it was not in him to do so. He was still in his early thirties, the incarnation of *La Grande Nation*, of its ascendancy and 'civilizing mission'. He had vast colonial ambitions and he aimed at world domination.

Had Bonaparte [writes an American historian] been content to consolidate France within the natural frontiers it had attained, while allowing the other powers comparable annexations, it is possible that the fifteen years war that followed might have been averted. But to secure the conquests of the Revolution . . . he insisted on transcending them. He sought to confirm and augment the ascendancy of France, and this meant keeping Europe in a state of disequilibrium. On Bonaparte, therefore, must rest the heaviest share of responsibility for the Napoleonic wars.

Talleyrand had wanted an alliance with Great Britain, for economically the two countries could complement each other and develop the world, with a constitutional monarchy on English lines for France. But the Peace of Amiens was a truce which ended before Napoleon meant it to. The British had been alarmed when the French, resuming their eighteenth-century colonial policy, had bought back Louisiana from Spain, sent an expedition to independent Haiti (San Domingo) since it was in the interest of civilization to destroy this 'new Algiers', dispatched troops to India to recover French trading ports and coasted south Australia which they called *Terre Napoléon*. Then, in 1803, Napoleon annexed Piedmont and Elba, sent troops to back the pro-French faction in Switzerland and became President of the Italian, formerly Cisalpine, Republic. The French were also active in the Ottoman Empire and seemed again to threaten Egypt; most significantly – and here was the essential point – they still kept control of Belgium and delayed their evacuation of Holland. In the long term, too, the British feared that they could build a fleet big enough to challenge their own. Evidently Napoleon's diplomacy was to be war by other means, and he was already excluding British goods from all the ports that he could.

Charles, Viscount Whitworth, the aristocrat whose cool insistence on English rights provoked Napoleon to rage.

So the British now delayed handing back Malta to the Knights, thus breaking the Treaty, and sent a particularly glacial ambassador to Paris. Lord Whitworth was a very tall Guardsman turned diplomat; as Ambassador to St Petersburg, he had already outfaced Catherine the Great, who had retaliated with the remark, 'Sir, since the King, your master, is determined to drive me from St Petersburg, I hope he will allow me to retire to Constantinople.' He had married the rich Dowager Duchess of Dorset, the owner of Knole Park, and they arrived in great style, the Ambassador instructed to insist on the British keeping Malta for ten years and that the French evacuate Holland and Switzerland.

So there was a memorable scene. This impassive embodiment of the English oligarchy particularly infuriated Napoleon: 'Talleyrand', he said afterwards, 'told me something that put me in a temper, and this great gawk of an ambassador came and put himself in front of my nose.' *'Malheurs'*, he yelled, *'Malheurs à ceux qui ne respectent pas les traités. Ils se seront responsables à toute l'Europe!'* ('Misfortune to those who do not respect treaties. They shall be responsible to all Europe!'); and then, in a marked manner, he left the room. Two hundred people, reported the pained Ambassador, heard this conversation, 'if such it could be called', and were shocked by 'the extreme impropriety of his conduct and the total want of dignity as well as decency on the occasion'. In spite of later civilities, the breach became entire.

On 18 May 1803 the British declared war, for it was not only Belgium but the hegemony of the continent that was in question. Once in the war, the British found many in the royalist resistance ready to try to assassinate the First Consul, and they subsidized their plots. The most spectacular came in February 1804. Georges Cadoudal, the Breton who had organized the attempt in the Rue Niçaise, was now financed by William Windham, Pitt's high-minded Secretary of State at War, and in collaboration with the Comte d'Artois, he had landed in France from an English brig and plotted with Generals Pichegru and Moreau to kill Napoleon on a ceremonial parade. Arrested, he confessed that the attempt was to coincide with the arrival of a Bourbon prince in Paris. The Comte d'Artois was the obvious man, but Napoleon could not get at him; but suspicion had fallen on a less important Bourbon-Condé collateral.

The Duc d'Enghien lived at Ettelheim in Baden, more concerned about sport and love affairs than conspiracies. But Napoleon could reach him, and he 'needed a Bourbon'; not just in the way of vendetta but to prove that once and for all he would never come to terms with them; that he was still in that respect the Revolution incarnate and its natural representative. He was determined both to fulfil a vendetta and win the throne himself. So in March 1804 he sent *gendarmes* to violate the frontier of Baden, kidnap the convenient victim by night and bring him at once to Vincennes. Compromising papers were naturally discovered, though nothing connected d'Enghien with the Cadoudal plot. But the judicial murder had been coldly planned. Before a military tribunal, d'Enghien protested that a Condé could return to revolutionary France only 'under arms'. He was shot at 2.30 a.m. within the hour; his grave had been dug beforehand and he was denied a priest. The methods of the *maquis* had been brought to an inter-national level.

Throughout the Courts of Europe there was horror and disgust. Who would now be safe? Beethoven cancelled the dedication of the *Eroica* Symphony to the First Consul. Napoleon, his own life threatened, had reciprocated in kind: 'My blood is worth as much as theirs.' But there was more in it than that. 'It was a sacrifice', he would say, 'necessary to my safety and my greatness.'

92

The next move was plain: all could no longer depend on Napoleon's life and a new dynasty must be founded for France. Then, if Napoleon were killed, the country would not relapse into Jacobin anarchy or a Bourbon White Terror; the owners of the Church lands would feel safe; all who had done well out of the Revolution would keep their gains, the bourgeoisie and the richer peasants feel more secure. So the generals, the senators, the politicians were sounded out; various kites were flown. France was, after all, accustomed to monarchy.

Josephine naturally opposed a project which, if Napoleon wanted direct heirs, implied her divorce. But the Council of State and the politicians and deputies approved, and a plebiscite gave the proposal overwhelming support. So, in May 1804, Napoleon was proclaimed Emperor of the French – *Imperator* like *Consul* was a classic Roman term. The Corsican adventurer would briefly occupy the throne of the Capets, the Valois and the Bourbons, but with a more vaulting ambition. He would now be not only founder of a new dynasty, but the Charlemagne *de nos jours*, an Emperor of the West.

The execution of the Duke d'Enghien.

93

We be the King's men, hale and hearty
Marching to meet one Bonaparte,
If he won't sail lest the wind do blow,
We shall have marched for nothing, O!

HARDY

5 Emperor of the West? 1804-8

NAPOLEON NOW DESTROYED the balance of power in Europe by asserting the complete ascendancy of France. *La Grande Nation*, with twenty-eight million inhabitants, would bring western and central Europe into one empire and the benefits of the Revolution to all its peoples – equality before the law, the career open to talents and to business enterprise. With this domination of France in Europe and of Europe in the world, world mastery would come about: a vast expansion of colonial settlement; the control of the Americas, of India and the Far East.

Yet this objective implied the command of the oceans, and that meant the conquest or the economic ruin of England. But here Napoleon confronted a nation so tenacious and realistic, with such overwhelming economic advantages – for there the Industrial Revolution had first been developed – and with so well-tried and professional a grasp of naval strategy and tactics, that he was outclassed. In 1798 he had written to the Directory from Egypt that fate had assigned to the French mastery of the land and to the English the mastery of the seas. That decree his ambition would now lead him to defy.

A vast contest now opened up: Tolstoi would describe it in *War and Peace*, the greatest novel ever written; Hardy in *The Dynasts* in a cosmic setting. Before the more monstrous and far-flung conflicts of our own century, it seemed the most spectacular war in history and it occasioned hideous carnage; but nothing so bestial as the mechanized holocausts of the Somme or so awful as the destruction of Dresden, Hiroshima and Nagasaki, so that the glamour of war, an institution still taken for granted, of splendid uniforms and fine horses, still hypnotized most opinion. The men of the Romantic age gloried in it.

In diplomacy, Napoleon showed a brilliant skill: one by one, he defeated and divided the Allies of the Third Coalition. In turn he broke the armies – though not the peoples – of Austria, Russia and Prussia, then of Russia again, so that they did not maintain concerted action until the Fourth and final Coalition. Only England stood out almost all through: save for the brief Peace of Amiens, England was at war from 1792 to 1814, and again in 1815.

The declaration of war in 1803 had been made because conditions would plainly be worse later, and Napoleon's letter to George III asking for peace as from one royalty to another, had been coldly answered: 'His Britannic Majesty must consult his Allies.' For it was no 'nation of shopkeepers' (a remark first made by the Corsican Paoli – '*sono mercanti*' which had a different ring)

PREVIOUS PAGES Jacques Louis David's well-known painting of the Coronation of the Emperor Napoleon and his Empress Josephine.

BELOW An English cartoon shows 'Little Johnny Bull' advancing on Napoleon to check his conquests.

A STOPPAGE to a STRIDE over the GLOBE

The Allies viewed Napoleon's progress with dismay but the cartoonists everywhere went to town.

LEFT Gillray's cartoon 'The King of Brobdingnag and Gulliver': George III and his Queen peer with amusement at Napoleon attempting to manœuvre his small boat in a basin of water.

BELOW The Allies thrust Napoleon into an oven with enthusiasm – the French view.

ABOVE A watercolour of the
battle of Austerlitz, by
Lejeune: Napoleon has
General Wimphen's wounds
dressed, after Lejeune, an
officer in Napoleon's army,
has taken the General
prisoner.

LEFT Gautier's watercolour of
Napoleon's camp at Boulogne,
strategically placed in preparation
for the invasion of England that
never took place. Instead, the scene
of combat moved back to Europe.

that Napoleon had challenged, but a hard-bitten, hard-drinking oligarchy backed by great wealth; by tough industrial entrepreneurs and a solid middle class, and in spite of poverty and social strife, by a populace with, on balance, a rising standard of living following the Industrial Revolution. Save in Ireland, the British had long damped down their old religious conflicts that had made them vulnerable in the seventeenth century, and, apart from Whig and Radical appeasers, an ancient and robust patriotism united most of them in loyalty to the throne and an insular contempt of foreigners. In the West, only in Spain was there a similar if darker xenophobia, but there it was not backed by political or economic strength but channelled in archaic institutions and clerical obscurantism. And in the East, in Russia, there was an even more massive, primitive and docile solidarity over territories that dwarfed western Europe, a recklessness of life that outmatched Napoleon's, and a winter climate as hostile as the wastes of the North Atlantic.

So the ten years' conflict began. In the end, the balance of power in Europe was restored, and it lasted until 1870-1 when the Germans would make an empire and begin their own attempt at the conquest and unification of Europe.

When, on 2 December 1804, Napoleon assumed an imperial crown in Notre Dame, with Pope Pius VII, like a chaplain, in attendance, he was consecrated, after he had rejected the title 'Emperor of the Gauls', not as King of France, but as Emperor of the French. It was an elaborate ceremony in which the Parisian flair for public splendour had full effect, and by 1808 the more reconcilable aristocrats of the *ancien régime* had to make the best of a new 'imperial' nobility. The grandeur of monarchy, deep in French tradition, was now refurbished in the lavish style in England called 'Regency', chastened in France by a neo-classical fashion. The synthetic ceremonial of the Republic was discarded and, though Napoleon refused to take the sacrament, a version of the old ritual was employed; but in Paris, not at Rheims, and Napoleon, with a studied and dramatic gesture, crowned himself.

For 'the most glorious and most august Emperor of the French' new emblems had been devised; the official one became the eagle in Roman style, though the claims of the lion and even the elephant had been canvassed; the personal emblem became the bee, since ornamental bees had been found in the tomb of the Merovingian Chilperic. Since Napoleon and Josephine had been

100

united only by a civil marriage, they were remarried, on Josephine's insistence, by Christian rites before the ceremony, at which Napoleon crowned his Empress; an episode, depicted by J. L. David, that made many nineteenth-century romantics weep. Madame Mère, now an Imperial Highness, was included in David's picture, but she did not, in fact, attend; she was in Rome with Lucien, now on bad terms with his brother. Napoleon also sent for his old nurse from Corsica to witness his fabulous elevation. Josephine and Louis rode with him in the state coach; they were on good enough terms for Napoleon to remark, as they stood in their fantastic finery, 'If only our father could see us now!' His sisters, conceded the title of Imperial Highness, disliked carrying Josephine's train, but in the end they acquiesced. There was a great parade of velvets and ermine, ostrich feathers and silks, the men as opulently got-up as the women. The whole impressive charade centred on an Emperor aged thirty-five; it delighted the more volatile Parisians, disgusted the high conservative aristocracy and was very good for the luxury trades.

In England, in ruling circles, the 'prevailing sentiment was one of amusement, restrained by an aristocratic and intellectual contempt' at 'this *singerie* [monkey business] of Charlemagne'. Officially Napoleon I remained, and would remain, General Bonaparte.

With success and relative security, the gaunt young General was beginning to grow sleek and plump. He was sensitive to his surroundings and to weather; he hated the cold; loved open fires and hot baths – he would often lie in one for an hour while the morning reports were read to him. He would always shave himself, a necessary precaution with the razors then in vogue and he always used English ones, and preferred Windsor soap: he took elaborate care to clean his teeth, which were very good; and, though he disliked strong scents, he doused his handkerchiefs in eau de cologne. He was, indeed, hypersensitive to smell, though he took a coarse snuff and detested the stuffy Paris interiors then in vogue: 'Open the windows', he would say, 'and I'll breathe God's air.' Napoleon needed little sleep and could take it at will. He had fits of rage, when he would overturn a table or stamp on his hat, but they were often calculated: when content, he would sing to himself, rather out of tune.

He liked to play with children and tell them creepy stories, but habitually cheated at cards. With all his luxury, he kept to a strict routine, and unlike most Frenchmen, took little time over his food.

ABOVE The home of
Napoleon and Josephine at
Malmaison where Josephine
indulged her passion for
gardening.

OPPOSITE Gérard's painting
of Napoleon in imperial
robes.

Dunon, then his *chef*, had little scope and the Emperor continued
to drink an indifferent and diluted Burgundy. He was considerate
to the servants, as, in pale blue coats and silver lace, they looked
after him in Louis XVI's former suite in the Tuileries. For himself,
he generally wore a plain dark green uniform coat over white
breeches, with silk stockings and buckled shoes; as on campaign
he wore his simple grey overcoat and low plain hat, contrasting
with the flamboyance of his entourage. Like all dictators, he must
have been lonely, for he ruled ultimately by fear.

Disillusioned after his romantic passion for Josephine, his
attitude to women had become more matter of fact. At St Helena
he would remark, 'We Westerners have spoilt everything by
treating women too well. We are quite wrong to make them
almost our equals. The Eastern peoples have been much more
sensible.' He was easy to flatter, *'naif avec des rouées'*, but never
allowed them political influence or much money. His most
scandalous affair while First Consul had been with Mlle Joséphine
('Georges') Weimar, *la belle tragédienne*, for at two in the morning,
in the Tuileries, Mlle 'Georges' was horrified to find that the
First Consul had been so carried away that he had fainted;
whereupon she quite lost her head, threw water over her lover
and rang every bell available. Servants arrived; then the other
Josephine, in her night dress. The First Consul recovered, Mlle
'Georges' made herself scarce and she was not received there again.

Josephine as Empress now became more wildly extravagant,
to the distress of her economical husband (she once bought

102

thirty-eight hats in a month); but their home at Malmaison at Rueil was intimate, elegant and relatively small. The Empress developed a passion for gardening and her Malmaison roses set new standards of texture, scent and size. She also accumulated a fine collection of pictures and a large menagerie. After the divorce, he would grudge her no expense for her gardens, and her botanists and collections were allowed through the English blockade. She remained intensely jealous of his infidelities, for he had a *rendezvous galante* in the Allée des Veuves (Widows' Row) and, during his long absences, she became *souffrante* and hypochondriac, taking the waters at Plombières and at Aix. But Napoleon would still report his military trijmphs to her with an engaging directness – as in his brilliant campaign of 1805 which knocked out first the Austrians, then the Russians, *'je suis en bonne position et je t'aime'* ('I am in a good position and I love you').

In May 1805, after a second coronation as the Sovereign of Italy, when Napoleon, *Rex Totius Italiae*, crowned himself with the Iron Crown of Lombardy, the most extraordinary year of all his adventures began. The gesture had in effect erased the Peace of Lunéville concluded with Austria. Already in April, an Anglo-Russian alliance had been signed at St Petersburg and the Third Coalition was in being. There is no doubt that Napoleon now seriously meant to invade England; he had concentrated 132,000 men at Boulogne and in August he wrote to Josephine about his riding and the view of the camp and sea. A flotilla of two thousand craft had been assembled: 'Let me be master of the Straits', he wrote, 'for six hours and we shall be masters of the world.' Like Hitler, he did not obtain either ambition.

His strategic plan had been sound; if it had demanded too much in execution and timing over so vast an area of the Atlantic. For by 1805 Napoleon had a new ally: England had declared war on Spain. Reviving a plan of the old regime in the naval archives, he therefore ordered Villeneuve, his admiral at Toulon, to break out of the Mediterranean in spite of Nelson's blockade and make right across the ocean for Martinique in the West Indies, now restored to France. Here a Spanish squadron and the French Atlantic fleet under Admiral Ganteaume, which was to break out of Brest in Brittany; Rochefort behind Oleron; and from Ferrol in Galicia, would combine. This formidable concentration would threaten the valuable British West Indies, and the British would send their main power to deal with it. Villeneuve was then to recross the Atlantic at speed and so, sailing up Channel, win command of the Straits for the swift crossing of the invasion force at Boulogne.

At first the ambitious strategy went well. Villeneuve, in March, evaded Nelson, and by May he was in Martinique. But Nelson was now after him, and Ganteaume, still blocked by the English, had not put to sea: the essential conjunction had not been made. So Villeneuve made for Ferrol in Spain. But one of Nelson's frigates had brought intelligence to the Admiralty of his course, and Admiral Calder, blockading Ushant in Brittany, sailed south and deflected him to Corunna, which faces Ferrol from the south. The English Channel fleet had thus refused the lure of the West Indies: only Nelson, with the Mediterranean fleet, had gone there. But Nelson, having returned to Gibraltar, now sailed north to join Calder's ships. Napoleon ordered Villeneuve to break out of Ferrol and join Ganteaume at Brest, and in mid-August he got out; but seeing French battleships out of Rochefort, he mistook them for Nelson's ships of the line and, with sickness aboard, turned tail right down to Cadiz. He had, in fact, abdicated from the Channel enterprise and not even gone back to Toulon, a French base. The essential strategy, like that of the Armada, had collapsed.

Napoleon, in furious exasperation, waiting with his great army near Boulogne, now realized that the game was up. Villeneuve was trapped in Cadiz, and soon Trafalgar would turn the English victory from a defensive strategic success to the entire command of the oceans. Already, that September, George III in Gloucester Lodge at Weymouth could watch through 'the open window . . . the crescent curved expanse of the Bay as a sheet of translucent green, on which are vessels of war at anchor', and know that his realm was secure.

The British had not only put paid to the invasion; they would now attack: they had long been pouring out subsidies and would spend six and a half million pounds on the Coalitions; massive Austrian and Russian forces were being concentrated to clear north Germany, Holland and Switzerland of the French, and – the main objective – drive them out of Italy by an attack on Lombardy and on Naples. By mid-August Napoleon had already dictated the plan for a lightning stroke against Vienna to knock out the Austrians, then turn on the Russians and Austrians in Bohemia before Prussia entered the conflict. And this he did, dealing with his enemies one after the other in the most brilliant of all his campaigns. All depended on speed: by 16 August the

The magnificent palace of Schönbrunn where Napoleon contemplated his next move after Ulm.

army at Boulogne was marching hard for the Rhine.

Early in September, the Austrian General Mack, with sixty thousand men, had advanced into Bavaria and occupied Ulm on the Upper Danube, well placed to block an invasion by the usual route through the Schwarzwald. But Napoleon after concentrating his armies from Boulogne at Mainz and from Hanover at Würzburg, soon had 190,000 men; then he humbugged the Austrians by a pretended attack through the Schwarzwald, but in fact brought his main force round north of it and so down to envelop Ulm and cut its communication with Vienna. Mack was hemmed inside the ancient walled city under the high spire of its cathedral. Then Napoleon followed strategic surprise by tactical victory as, in vile weather, the French stormed the heights of the Michaelsburg. On 20 October Mack capitulated with fifty thousand men.

Napoleon wrote to Josephine, 'I'm going to march against the Russians. They are done for. I am satisfied with my armies.'

106

By 4 November, though he had failed to bring the Russians to battle as they advanced to relieve Ulm, Napoleon, marching through the snow, was in Vienna. Installed on the outskirts in the elegant palace of Schönbrunn, he sized up the situation at once. The Russian Kutúzov's army was still intact, the French communications were extended, the grip on north Germany was impaired and, if the Prussians were to strike, Napoleon would be at serious risk. Determined to deal with the Russians at once, he advanced north from Vienna towards Brunn (Brno) tempting the main Russian armies, now linked up with the Austrians, to battle. Against Kutúzov's advice, the young Tsar Alexander Pávlovich fell into the trap.

Tolstoi has described in incomparable pages the Russian catastrophe at Austerlitz (now Slakov) between Brunn and the Morava. Early on 2 December, in icy fog which had cleared only on the higher ground, Napoleon closed the trap.

It was nine o'clock in the morning. The fog lay unbroken like a sea down below, but higher up . . . where Napoleon stood with his marshals around him it was quite light. Above him was a clear blue sky: and the sun's vast orb quivered like a huge, hollow, crimson float on the surface of that silky sea of mist. . . . His gleaming eyes were fixed intently on one spot. His predictions were being justified. Part of the Russian force had already descended into the valley . . . and part were leaving those Pratzen heights which he intended to attack and which he regarded as the key to the position.

Lured by a pretended retreat, the Russians and their Allies, over-riding the protests of Kutúzov, had tried to pursue the French right, which they thought was retiring, but which was in fact concealed by the fog and close up to them. They thus exposed their flank and even committed the staggering mistake of descending from the Pratzen heights which commanded the battle-field. Napoleon placed his artillery upon the heights and the French, emerging from the fog, smashed the Russian and Austrian armies. The Tsar and the Russians had been cleared out of central Europe.

'L'armée Russe', wrote Napoleon to Josephine, 'est non seulement battue, mais detruite' ('The Russian army is not only beaten but destroyed'); it was 'the finest [la plus belle] action in which I've ever engaged'. Forty-five standards, 150 cannon, twenty general officers were taken. Out of eighty-seven thousand of the enemy, he had accounted for twenty-seven thousand and all for eight thousand casualties out of seventy-three thousand Frenchmen.

Napoleon's troops bivouacking on the eve of Austerlitz: painted by Lejeune.

OVERLEAF A detail from Gros's painting of the battle of Eylau, now in the Louvre. The battle was fought in a snow-storm on 8 February 1807.

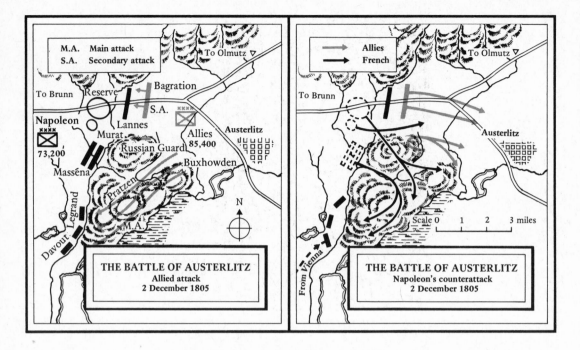

THE BATTLE OF AUSTERLITZ
Allied attack
2 December 1805

THE BATTLE OF AUSTERLITZ
Napoleon's counterattack
2 December 1805

'At last', he concluded, sincerely or for the benefit of public opinion, 'peace is restored to the continent. We must hope that it will be restored to the world. The English will not now be able to stand up to us.' The Austrian Emperor asked for an armistice and on 27 December Napoleon concluded 1805 by dictating the Treaty of Pressburg.

The Austrians had again to surrender all Venetia, Istria, Dalmatia and, what was much worse, Tyrol and the Vorarlberg. Their domination had now been removed from all Italy, and this time from south Germany as well, for Bavaria, Württemburg and Baden were set up as independent states. The Prussians now trimmed their sails, and by the Treaty of Schönbrunn, for the price of Hanover, gave up Anspach and Neuchâtel in Switzerland. The strategic significance even of Trafalgar seemed dwarfed by this continental transformation.

The Prussian rulers had been playing a dangerous game. In return for the great prize of Hanover and for the banishment of Austrian influence from south Germany, they had agreed to abolish the ancient Holy Roman Empire and to Napoleon's dominating the Germanies, now embodied in the Confederation of the Rhine. By February 1806, Napoleon made them give up part of the strategic

112

duchy of Cleves and agree to boycott English goods; and when, in the course of the peace negotiations initiated by Fox after Pitt's death, it looked as if Napoleon would sacrifice Hanover for recognition of his brother Joseph as King of Naples and Sicily, the Prussians were terrified that, in a general settlement, they might after all be sacrificed to Russia. So belatedly, on 7 October, in alliance with Russia, Sweden and Great Britain, King Frederick William III declared war. It was an insane decision, and Napoleon took immediate advantage of it.

The Prussian army was very large, two hundred thousand men,

One of Napoleon's proclamations to his soldiers expressing his confidence in them and urging them to greater glories, written from the camp at Austerlitz.

and it still had the prestige of Frederick the Great's victories; but it was also still fighting in the old cumbrous style, with elderly generals and many mercenaries. Naturally the military experts thought it invincible. The Prussians did not even wait for Russian reinforcements, but advanced south-west with 130,000 men to threaten the Rhineland and Napoleon's communications with France. So the Emperor riposted by striking north-east from Bamberg, north of Nürnberg, to threaten Berlin. The Prussians then retreated to protect their capital, and a week after the declaration of war, they were totally defeated at Jena east of Weimar by Napoleon, whose cavalry chased the fugitives through the city; then by Davout at Auerstadt. By 25 October the French had occupied Berlin, the King and Queen had fled right up to Königsberg (now Kaliningrad, USSR) on the Baltic beyond the Gulf of Danzig and then on to Memel. 'I am wonderfully well', wrote Napoleon to Josephine, 'I find *Sans Souci* [the palace of Frederick the Great] very agreeable.' He sent the Prussian King's sword and standards back to Paris. Rossbach had been avenged.

Napoleon now dictated harsh terms, depriving Frederick William III of half his territories and over five million of his subjects. Talleyrand, who had suffered much discomfort jolting over ghastly roads to follow his master, thought this policy utterly misguided. For the Emperor had now, as over the Austrian peace, disregarded his opinion that he should maintain the two great central European powers as a counterweight to Russia. Napoleon had crippled Prussia, but could not exterminate it, and it would spring up again with added ferocity as a militant great power.

Napoleon now planned a final attack on Russia, his third continental adversary, and promulgated the Berlin Decrees boycotting British goods from all the ports under his control on the entire European coastline from the eastern Baltic to southern Portugal and the Mediterranean. He was even now contemplating sending his armies through Spain to coerce the Portuguese. He was thus already, in 1806, set on the two ambitions that would bring him down – the coercion of Russia and of the Iberian peninsula. That was why Talleyrand wrote: 'I swore tonight that I would cease to be his [Foreign] Minister.'

Napoleon now faced a campaign in the depth of winter on the marches of north-eastern central Europe. In spite of their defeat at Austerlitz, the Russians had moved heavily into Poland and East Prussia, and at Pultusk, north of Warsaw, on 26 December,

The battle of Jena at which
the Prussians were defeated
on 14 October 1806, a
prelude to the occupation of
Berlin by Napoleon.

they had fought off a French attack. And when, in February 1807, at Eylau south of Königsberg, in an appalling battle fought partly in a thick snowstorm, the Grand Army inflicted forty thousand casualties on the Russians, the French suffered worse losses than hitherto incurred in any of Napoleon's campaigns. The Russians, under the German Bennigsen, had fought with stubborn bravery – they had been told that Napoleon had 'sold himself to the Jews and claimed to be the Messiah' and they had set new standards of slaughter and died where they stood. Their artillery, masked by the snow flurries, had proved devastating. It was almost a drawn battle and the French went ruefully into winter quarters.

But on 14 June, in the long days of the Baltic summer, with better visibility, Napoleon trapped another great Russian army at Friedland as he marched on Königsberg along the River Alle, parallel with the Russians on the other bank. For when the Russian commander Bennigsen attacked the city across the river, Napoleon, by a swift encirclement, shut him up in the town. Coralled in the burning city with the bridges over the Alle destroyed, another twenty-five thousand Russians were accounted for. Unfortunately for Napoleon, there were still a great many more.

'My army', he wrote, for he was now enjoying the war, 'is superb.' And the battle had been fought on 14 June; 'My children', wrote the Emperor, for thus he now thought of his soldiers, 'have worthily celebrated the anniversary of Marengo.' So he issued a proclamation to the Army: 'From the banks of the Vistula to those of the Niemen, we have come with the speed of an eagle. . . . Frenchmen, you have been worthy of yourselves and of myself.'

After the defeat of the Austrians at Ulm, of the Austrians and Russians at Austerlitz, of the Prussians at Jena and the Russians at Friedland, the Grand Army was now the terror of Europe. The nucleus of the armies was the Imperial Guard, a self-contained mobile striking-force of all arms. In the Napoleonic war of movement, the culmination of improved eighteenth-century techniques, they were decisive. Muskets had not been improved, but field guns were lighter and artillery mass-produced. Improved roads often made large-scale manœuvres practicable, and when the enemy had been out-manœuvred, the Guard would go in and decide the battle.

The Tsar had to ask for an armistice, and soon Napoleon was writing to Josephine, 'Alexander has more sense than is usually thought'; but in fact he had more sense than Napoleon thought, for he was playing for time. The two of them met on a raft on the

Niemen, a scene well evoked by Hardy: 'A multitude of soldiery and spectators line each bank of the broad river which, stealing north-west, bears almost exactly in its midst a moored raft of bonded timber. On this as a floor, stands a gorgeous pavilion of draped woodwork, having at each side, facing the opposite banks of the stream, a round-headed doorway richly festooned. The cumbersome erection acquires from the current a rhythmical movement, as if it were breathing, and the breeze now and then produces a shiver on the face of the stream.'

The Tsar was apparently fascinated by Napoleon; but since the Russians detested the French, he feared a palace revolution if he came to a full alliance with them. And the alliance, even as made, was very unpopular in Russia: 'There were sermons against Antichrist . . . one peasant solved the problem of the reconciliation happily as follows: "The Tsar met Antichrist on a raft, in order to baptize him and at once before he had anything more to do with him."' In fact, Napoleon was duped. He had sent for the King and Queen of Prussia from Memel: 'The Tsar and the King of Prussia dine with me', he informed Josephine, 'and the charming Queen of Prussia.' But the adventurer was merely accepted, as royalty knew how to accept such people, and 'to the unhappy King of Prussia' Alexander appears to have said 'Wait, you will get it all

The famous meeting of Napoleon and Tsar Alexander on the raft on the Niemen: a cartoon by Gillray.

117

back. He will break his neck.' When in 1814 he entered Paris, the Tsar would remark 'And yet they thought I was a simpleton.'

The Russians, of course, got what they could out of the bargain. In 1806 the Sultan Selim, nominally an ally of France, had been overthrown, and the Russians now had a free hand to attack Turkey at a very convenient time. They also got a free hand in Finland, which they would annex in 1808 at the expense of Sweden and the Finns.

The Poles were of course 'betrayed'. Napoleon 'did not want to be their Don Quixote' and the Grand Duchy of Warsaw, carved mainly out of Prussian territory, was a poor substitute for a larger state. Jerome Bonaparte now became King of Westphalia, with its coastline linking up with Louis's kingdom of Holland, and better enforcing the blockade against England as well as the French control of the Confederation of the Rhine. The construction indeed appeared imposing, but British seapower remained predominant and would remain so; after the death of the appeasing Fox early in 1806, the English, to quote the French historian Sorel, again began to show the 'qualities of a sly and obstinate bull dog which are revealed in all Englishmen when the interests of England are at stake'.

Napoleon now began to think of securing a direct hereditary successor. He knew that, in spite of his failure to have an heir by Josephine, he could found a dynasty; for during the bitter Polish campaigns of the winter of 1806-7, at his first coming to Warsaw, he had met at a ball a young Polish beauty of dazzling charm, who of all his women he would love most, after his original passion for Josephine. Marie Walewska was a blue-eyed blonde with a skin of dazzling whiteness, sensitive, intelligent, with a *'coquetterie discrète'*. Moreover, in the best tradition of French opera, she was married to an elderly Count Alexander Walewski, allegedly a 'dotard' (*'sacrificiée à un vieillard imbécile'*). Napoleon was instantly attracted. He sent Duroc, one of his more sophisticated marshals, 'as the postillion of his master's love' to present to her his *'hommages et admiration'*. Dazzled and in fact hooked, the lovely girl decided to capitulate, but with the honours of war. She replied, with Polish fire, that she had nothing to say to him. Napoleon became extremely annoyed, the more so as his staff were boasting of their amatory conquests. In long and intimate letters, he poured out his feelings – *'l'impatient ardeur de N'*. 'O come, come,' he wrote, 'all your wishes shall be fulfilled. Your country will be the more dear to me when you take pity on

OPPOSITE Robert Lefebvre's portrait of Marie Walewska, the beautiful Polish girl whom Napoleon loved most after Josephine.

118

my poor heart.' Summoned to his palace at between ten and eleven at night, she arrived weeping and surrendered.

It was now even more important to prevent the Empress from joining her husband, and Napoleon wrote to Josephine, 'In the deserts of Poland one thinks little of lovely women.' He described the balls and routs of Warsaw, but for him always, he reiterated, there was only one woman. 'Do you know who it is? The nights seem long when one is alone.' The Empress was fended off and Napoleon is said to have shown the letters which prevented her arrival to his new mistress.

Count Walewski, like Lieutenant Fourès, now repudiated his wife, who that April joined Napoleon for three weeks in his headquarters at the fine château of Finkenstein. With Polish passion, she now adored him; though the soldiery, suffering the hardships of the campaign, remarked when she drove out with the Emperor, *c'est une vendue* – a bought woman.' The campaign soon parted them: but on 4 May 1807 at Walewitz and about six weeks before Tilsit, Marie Walewska had a son, Alexandre. In the press of business, the affair would fade, but Napoleon loved her and she him. When, after his abdication, he was living in diminished state on Elba, Marie Walewska would secretly present the four-year-old boy to his father. Napoleon would be delighted with the fair, curly-haired child, and 'play hide and seek and roll in the grass with him'. 'A little bird', he said, 'tells me that you never mention my name in your prayers.' 'That's true', replied Alexandre, 'I don't say Napoléon, I say *Papa Empéreur.'* Napoleon laughed and told Marie, 'He'll be a social success that one, he's got wit.'

At Tilsit, Napoleon had created an imperial nobility of service of continental range, designed to give his principal supporters an interest in a vast cosmopolitan regime. As he wrote to Joseph in Naples, Joseph's realm now touched the Mediterranean, Napoleon's the Baltic; and over all these territories he was determined to abolish the old class distinctions, eradicate the relics of serfdom, abolish mendicancy, bring equal rights to the Jews, rationalize the penal code and establish open courts of justice and trial by jury. But the mass of the people were not yet interested in such enlightened eighteenth-century-style reform, particularly when imposed by foreign conquerors.

And Napoleon now had even more problems in mind. After Tilsit, he retired to Dresden, where he wrote to Talleyrand 'We must concern ourselves soon with closing the Portuguese ports to the English.' He had also threatened to 'reduce the Pope to the status of any other bishop in my states', and asserted 'I hold my crown from God and the Will of My peoples.' Back in Paris, he accepted splendid furs from the Tsar and reciprocated with a set of Sèvres china. That October, he was hunting a great deal, and much concerned with making canals in France – Dijon-Paris, Rhône-Saône; in the Low Countries, Rhine-Scheldt; but in July the English had bombarded Copenhagen and captured the Danish fleet, and in December they would intensify their blockade. The conflict with the Pope worsened; in February 1808 the French had to occupy Rome and by April eighty thousand men were being mobilized to enter the Iberian peninsula. On 19 April Napoleon declared 'the interest of my House and of my Empire demand that the Bourbons cease to occupy the throne of Spain'. 'I don't want to harm anyone,' he observed, 'but when my great car of policy is launched, it must pass. Woe to those who find themselves beneath its wheels!'

The peace which Napoleon may by now have wished for his Empire, whatever his subconscious desires, still remained a mirage. At Erfurt that September Talleyrand would sum up the essentials: 'The French people', he would tell the Tsar, 'are civilized, their Emperor is not.'

6 The Brittle Greatness 1808-12

They have all given each other a rendezvous at my tomb.
But they dare not turn up.

NAPOLEON

AT THE MEETING WITH ALEXANDER I at Erfurt in 1808 Napoleon appeared at the summit of his power, with a retinue of subservient monarchs and of princes and dukes of his Empire. But beneath the pomp and glitter, the alliance had long been wearing thin; 'obstinate as a mule', the Tsar would not understand that if Napoleon relaxed his military grip, 'Europe would treat him as a little boy.' He still tried to dazzle Alexander by prospects in central Asia. More realistically, that summer, he had concentrated great armies at Mainz and Strasbourg, for the Austrian Court were planning their revenge. While at Erfurt Napoleon discussed with the Tsar the way to break the English blockade and 'restore the freedom of the seas', his domination of Europe was already being undermined: there was the growing conflict with the Pope; the steady if covert hatred of the Austrian and Prussian rulers, and a new and grave entanglement in Spain and Portugal, where, for the first time, the English had found a substantial foothold on the Continent. 'This devilment in Spain', Napoleon remarked at Erfurt, 'costs me dear.'

Talleyrand, his decision taken, was now regularly meeting Alexander, after the Conference, in the drawing-room of the Princess of Thurn and Taxis. From 1807 he had been doing 'all in his power to thwart Napoleon's ambitions and hasten his downfall' and Erfurt was the turning-point in the history of the Empire; Talleyrand was convinced that 'For the good of France and for the good of Europe Napoleon's power had to be destroyed.' He had been promoted – or kicked upstairs – to be Vice-Grand Elector, the third greatest office in the Empire; yet he was passing on Napoleon's secrets to the Tsar to whom he became, in fact, adviser: 'the last service', he wrote, 'that I was able to render to Europe as long as Napoleon continued to reign, and a service which, in my opinion, I rendered to him as well'. He still hoped to bring Napoleon to moderate his ambitions and consolidate a peaceful regime in France, for like others who had made a great fortune out of the Empire, he then had no wish for a Bourbon restoration.

With central Europe restive and the Russian alliance increasingly unreliable, Napoleon had been lured into the dangerous commitment in the Iberian peninsula. He had two reasons for intervention – to enforce the boycott against England, and to exploit the resources of Spain and Portugal, perhaps even of their American colonies. The excuse was the Portuguese failure to enforce the

PREVIOUS PAGES The entry into Paris of the Imperial Guard through the Austerlitz Arch in 1807, painted by Taunay.

124

blocus continental against British goods; the occasion, the disreputable intrigues at the Spanish Court which allowed the French to secure a passage through the country to Portugal. The Spanish royalties, as depicted in Goya's *Family of Carlos IV*, painted at Aranjuez in 1800, were both degenerate and disreputable: Carlos IV was not ill-meaning, but almost imbecile; his son, Fernando, Prince of Asturias, more malignantly stupid, evidently roused Goya's greatest contempt; and Queen Maria Luisa has the countenance of a harridan in a slum, all the more evil when set off by her finery. Godoy, her lover, originally

Goya's paintings of Carlos IV of Spain (*left*) and Maria Luisa of Palma, his wife and Queen (*right*). Napoleon shared the artist's critical perception of them and was disgusted by the entire royal family.

Fernando VII: an engraving from a painting by Lacoma. Of him Napoleon wrote: 'He has not yet said a word; he is indifferent to everything, very materialistic, eats four times a day and has no ideas of anything.'

promoted from the Royal Guard and incongruously called the Prince of Peace, wanted to oust the heir, Fernando. Both factions were bidding for French support.

In the autumn of 1807 Napoleon had thus been able to make the secret Treaty of Fontainebleau whereby Portugal would be partitioned and compelled to enforce the blockade, and whereby French troops would enter Spain. So when a French army had occupied Portugal, though the Portuguese King and Queen and fleet had escaped to Brazil, French troops had occupied strategic positions in Spain, ostensibly to secure their communications. So in the spring of 1808, Godoy had persuaded the Spanish Bourbons to imitate Louis XVI and flee the country as had the Portuguese royalties, and the Spaniards at Aranjuez had risen in revolt against Carlos IV and Godoy. Napoleon had then seized his chance; Murat, with a large army, was already in Spain, and

126

in April 1808 Napoleon, who now had the whip hand, had summoned the King, the Queen, Fernando and Godoy to a conference at Bayonne where Napoleon brilliantly summed them up. He did not mind the old King, but found the Prince of Asturias 'very stupid, malicious and an enemy of France. . . . The queen has her love life [*cœur*] and her past written on her physiognomy – that says enough!' They were 'worse than you could imagine', and the Prince of Peace was 'like a bull'.

Their position was technically peculiar. Carlos IV had abdicated in favour of Fernando, and then rescinded his decision; but Fernando VII still claimed to be King. Napoleon made a clean sweep of them all: Fernando was forced to resign the throne to his father, who had already resigned his rights to Napoleon; the King and Queen were deported to France, then to Italy. Fernando and his brother Carlos were detained in luxurious captivity in France, where they made a bonfire of the works of Voltaire and Rousseau, and one of them killed time by making wolf traps. The field was clear for another Bonaparte. Already in March Napoleon had alerted his brother Louis, King of Holland, that he would be needed as King of Spain. But Louis had firmly refused;

An engraving showing the capture of Godoy after the riots at Aranjuez in 1808.

Napoleon's brother Joseph with his wife Julie. Napoleon substituted them for the deposed Bourbon royal family in Spain.

so Joseph was summoned from Naples and Sicily, where he was replaced by Caroline and her husband Murat, and in June Joseph arrived in his new kingdom.

This outrage infuriated the Spaniards. When the royalties had left for Bayonne, there had been an insurrection in Madrid; now Saragossa revolted. Spontaneously the Spaniards formed provincial *Juntas* to organize a savage resistance. Undeterred, Napoleon ordered General Dupont's division to push on to the extreme south and seize Cadiz, but this risky move had its reward. Surrounded in July by superior Spanish forces at Baylen, east of Cinares where the railway now turns north to Madrid, Dupont had to conclude a convention whereby he evacuated his army; whereat the *Junta* at Seville had repudiated the deal and thrown his men into prison. '*Bête, Imbécile, Poltron*' ('Beast, fool, coward'), commented Napoleon: it was not only a defeat, it was a disgrace.

And, what was worse, the English had promptly intervened. In August 1808 they had defeated Junot and the Army of Portugal

128

at Vimiero on the coast thirty miles above Lisbon and forced him to accept the Convention of Cintra. 'The army', said Napoleon, 'is commanded not by generals but by Inspectors of the Posts.' So on 18 September 1808, nine days before Erfurt, he had issued a proclamation: 'Soldiers, I need you! The hideous presence of the *Leopard* sullies the continents of Spain and Portugal: at the sight of you if will fly in panic. Let us carry our eagles to the Pillars of Hercules!' The *Leopard* would not panic, and to its natural verve it would add tenacity.

After Erfurt, Napoleon returned to Paris. By December, for the first and last time, he was in Spain, where he abolished feudal obligations, suppressed provincial barriers, turned out the Inquisition and abrogated many other cherished old Spanish customs. Most Spaniards clung to them all – and practically all Spaniards detested the French, from the upstart Bonaparte and the 'intrusive' King downwards. But Napoleon had the troops of the Guard with him, and Sir John Moore, who had advanced north-east to Burgos to attack the French supply-lines to Bayonne, was nearly caught when the Emperor cut his communications with Portugal at Salamanca and advanced to encircle him while Soult contained him at Burgos. Hence one of those retreats which have passed into British folk lore as a kind of victory; and indeed, since Napoleon left Soult to finish them off, most of the army escaped to Corunna, where 'not a drum was heard nor a funeral note' at the celebrated interment of their general.

But the English still commanded the sea and they still held Portugal; as is their habit, they came back again, and in the spring of 1809 Sir Arthur Wellesley was appointed to another European command. Napoleon's empire had now met its most redoubtable enemy on land, the one personally of all Napoleon's adversaries the most dramatically contrasted with him. The small British expeditionary force, never more than thirty thousand men, supplied by sea, were pitted against two hundred thousand French, who also had to contend not only with the Spanish and Portuguese regular armies, but with the spontaneous *guerrilla* warfare congenial to the Spaniards (*guerrillero* is a Spanish term), a long-drawn war of ambushes and throat-slitting and stringing-up; the 'ulcer' of Napoleon's empire, a fit subject for the macabre side of Goya's genius.

In February 1809, Napoleon wrote to Joseph 'I hope that this year Europe will again be at peace. I hope so little that yesterday

I signed a decree to call up 100,000 men.' At the end of January
he arrived back in Paris 'like a thunderbolt': he attacked Fouché
and summoned a meeting of the Great Council when he subjected
Talleyrand to half an hour's tirade. 'You are a thief', he shouted,
'a coward, a man without honour, you don't believe in God,
nothing is sacred to you . . . you would sell your own father . . .
you deserve that I should smash you like a glass but I despise
you too much to take the trouble. You are dung in a silk stocking.'
Unperturbed, the Vice-Grand Elector afterwards remarked:
'What a pity that such a great man should be so ill bred.' But
Napoleon had abandoned the Machiavellian precept that when
you strike, you destroy: Talleyrand remained in office.

Napoleon had reason to be concerned; the Austrians now
were ready for war and he had quickly to reorganize his massive
striking power. By the end of March 1809 he had concentrated
eighty thousand men at Ratisbon on the Lech and on 9 April
Austria declared war. Eight days later, Napoleon was with his
army, 'I have decided', he wrote, 'to exterminate the army of
Prince Charles' then attacking the city; 'Activité! Activité!
Vitesse!' he urged on Masséna. Like lightning, he struck into
Bavaria and at Landshutt and at Eckmuhl he inflicted resounding
defeats on the Austrians. So in May 1809 he was again in Vienna,
and issuing from Schönbrunn his decree as Emperor of the
French, King of Italy and Protector of the Confederation of the
Rhine, that the Papal States were now 'reunited' with the French
Empire, 'since our predecessor Charlemagne had given them to
the Bishop of Rome but had kept them part of his dominions'.
The Pope now excommunicated Napoleon, for there was nothing
much else he could do, and Napoleon had him deported to Savona.

A large Austrian army was still intact across the Danube
menacing Vienna; so Napoleon occupied the island of Lobau, and
when the Archduke sent heavy barges down-stream to smash the
bridge, French engineers shored it up. Napoleon then launched
his sanguinary and indecisive attack on Aspern-Essling and the
bridge was again smashed behind him; but he held on to the
island, protected by an improvised flotilla, and repaired it.
Reinforced by Eugène's army from Italy which had defeated the
Austrians at Raab, he now disposed of 180,000 men and, early in
July, again crossed the Danube and attacked the Austrians at
Wagram. They over-extended themselves and he smashed their
centre with an overwhelming attack in column backed by massive
artillery.

The Austrian Empire was now, it seemed, finally crippled, and by the Peace of Schönbrunn lost all the Illyrian provinces, Salzburg and a slice of Galicia, and was subjected to a swingeing indemnity. It had been a brilliant campaign, if the casualties on both sides had been severe, and at Schönbrunn, which he always liked, Napoleon had been in great form. He particularly enjoyed the crystalline water of a spring in the park: 'Do you like fresh water?' he asked one of his colonels. *'Ma foi'*, came the reply, 'I'd rather have a good glass of Bordeaux or Champagne!' 'Send the colonel', the Emperor ordered, 'a hundred bottles of each.' His sense of public relations had never been sharper.

But there was the usual bad news from Spain. The English, he said, were the only people there who could fight, and if things went on in this way, there would be a catastrophe. In Germany, too, Jerome, King of Westphalia, had shown notable incompetence.

Then in August the English landed on Walcheren at the mouth of the Scheldt, though they did little good for themselves. Most significant, the peoples of the restive Empire were now behind their governments; a fact symbolized by the attempt of a German student, Friedrich Staps, to knife Napoleon. He was the son of a Lutheran pastor, brought up on Christian principles; but he went to his execution crying out 'Long live Germany! Death to the Tyrant.' As Rohan Butter records in *The Roots of National Socialism*, he was representative of a surge of Germanic nationalism, most formidable in Prussia, where in 1807 Fichte had given his lectures *On the Chief Differences between the Germans and the other Peoples of Teutonic Descent*. The Germans, he had said, are an *Urfolk*, the one people who have the right to call itself a *'Volk'* – nation. In 1806 Ludwig von Arnim had been writing of 'consecrated daggers', and in 1809 Kleist wrote *Germania and her Children*, 'of all German battle songs perhaps the most terrible in sheer delight in carnage':

> Dost thou arise, Germania?
> Is the day of vengeance here?

Her children were 'Scions of the cohort stormers, the brood that overcame the Romans! *Enkel der Kohortenstürmer, Romerüberwinderbrut!'* They should hunt down the Frenchman as the marksman tracks the wolf and 'strike him dead – *Schlagt ihn tot'*.

Against this sort of thing, the eighteenth-century dynastic manœuvres whereby Napoleon hoped to pacify Europe looked outdated. But so he attempted to stabilize his dynasty. Rejected

131

Gros's painting of the battle
of Wagram in which
Napoleon crushed the
Austrians in 1809.

by the Romanovs, he now forced himself on the proud Hapsburgs and planned to marry the Archduchess Marie Louise, daughter of the Austrian Emperor. She could give him children and bring him into the heart of the great dynastic web of the old Europe. It would be an insurance even if his Empire collapsed.

But Josephine would have to go: by November 1809, Napoleon was resolute on this decision and, in truth, for all her casual charm and elegance, she had never really lived up to her position. 'I recommend to you that you show a little character and to learn how to put everyone in their places', he had written before Jena. He now gave out that he was making an agonizing sacrifice – God only knew what it cost him – and on 15 December the marriage of Napoleon and his first Empress was dissolved. An irregularity had been discovered in the ceremony before the Coronation; her parish priest had not been there. Josephine had taken it hard and fainted at table, though, when carried out, she had whispered 'Take care, you're holding me too tight.' She had then given way to a *funeste mélancholie*. Nor was Napoleon unmoved for, when he was there, they had reached a more harmonious domesticity at Malmaison. 'I was depressed', he wrote to her after the separation, 'to see the Tuileries, the great palace, deserted and empty and I felt lonely.' He presented her with a parure of rubies worth four hundred thousand francs, and told her that she would find another five hundred thousand 'in the cupboard at Malmaison'. He also gave her a hundred thousand francs to spend on her gardens; he saw her quite often and made her Duchess of Navarre, near Evreux in Normandy, with a large estate, servants and two million francs a year. But when, in March 1810, he married his Archduchess, Josephine's jealousy overcame her discretion, and she wrote in the third person with the most cutting formality to her former husband, demanding more money to settle her debts and to be put into possession of her duchy. Then she took refuge in taking the waters at Aix-les-Bains and bought a property near Vevey, while Napoleon told his people that they would find a *tendre mère* in the new Empress, though he complained to Fouché that the papers went on gossiping about Josephine.

The Hapsburgs had followed the ancient principle which had made their house – '*Bella gerant alii; tu, felix Austria, nube*'. ('Let others wage war; you, happy Austria, marry!'); they had sacrificed the young Archduchess to buy time. Napoleon, with his Corsican background, thought that these royalties, long accustomed to use their kin as pawns, would accept a clannish family solidarity and even sentiment. He was quite out of his depth.

The Tsar had kept studiedly aloof from the obligations of Tilsit and Erfurt, and, on the plea that the old Tsarina must decide, had avoided giving his sister to Napoleon; the Austrian marriage had been Napoleon's answer. The mirage of the Russian alliance was now vanishing, as Alexander already showed signs of veering towards Prussia, cowed though it still was. For Napoleon, beneath the apparent grandeur, 1810 was an anxious year; and by mid-summer he was asking 'What is Russia up to? Does it want war. I don't want to end my destiny in sands and deserts.'

On the face of it, his position had never been more magnificent. He had begun to make Paris a capital worthy of a European empire; created the Italianate arcades of the Rue de Rivoli, the Rues Castiglione and de la Paix; paved the *quais* by the Seine, and made three new bridges over it. He had the neo-Roman Arch of Austerlitz and the Arc de Triomphe put up, adorning the first with the splendid antique bronze horses stolen from St Mark's, Venice, returned after Waterloo; he also illuminated part of the city with the new 'gas' lamps. But he was wary of too much cult of himself and refused to rename the Place de la Concorde as Place Napoléon. Compared with twentieth-century dictators, he was modest.

His taste in art and sculpture was conventional and political; very well served by Ingres and David, with their stress on accuracy and finish. He liked historical subjects in painting, but they had to be records of success, and he remarked of David's *Thermopylae*, 'Not a suitable subject for painting. Leonidas lost.' When confronted with a group of naiads in a courtyard of the Louvre whose breasts were spouting water, he observed, 'Remove those wet nurses, the naiads were virgins.' Very much a man of the eighteenth century, Napoleon respected and encouraged the arts, but they had to be official. Perhaps his happiest influence was on furniture, when a certain neo-classic military austerity came in; a more dignified splendour contrasting with previous baroque fashions.

In literature, his taste remained basically classical, for he greatly admired the tragedies of Corneille, knew the *Iliad* well in translation and could even take the historical tragedies of Voltaire. But, like many men of his time, he was fascinated by Macpherson's *Ossian*, and by the maunderings as well as the insight of Rousseau.

135

His patronage of writers, dramatists and musicians could be lavish but conventional and killing. As a ruler of France, Italy and Germany, he understood the importance of subsidizing the opera and he appreciated Mozart's music; but his natural taste was for the more obvious tunefulness of Italian composers. Opera and the theatre flourished under the Empire better than innovating painters or writers. Napoleon's own choice of novels was also conventional, and indeed he liked rather cheap, unexacting stories which passed the time. His real passion was for reading history: he even read Gregory of Tours' *History of the Franks*, a miniature record of political murder which made his own more extensive political crimes seem tame.

Though Napoleon was a freethinker, he cared little for liberty of thought. The highly centralized system of state *lycées* was extended during the Empire, and the teachers regarded as the servants of the state. The private schools and Catholic-controlled seminaries were penalized, for he wanted to give the state education an increasing monopoly, directed to the deliberate inculcation of ideas and attitudes which would support his regime, which on the face of it then appeared successful.

For the climax of the Empire, with its brief phases of precarious continental peace, enabled the richer Parisians to enjoy the plunder of Europe, and a hectic prosperity masked the miseries of the life of the populace, particularly acute during the near famines of 1812.

By 1810, with Austria subdued, it was Napoleon's fixed intention to stabilize the situation, and had it not been for the war with England, which implied intensifying the blockade, and the war in Spain, he might perhaps have done so. Early in February he had asked for the hand of the Archduchess, giving Schwarzenberg, the Austrian ambassador, only a day for his decision. Instructed from Vienna for this contingency, Schwarzenberg had at once accepted on behalf of his master. For Francis II and Metternich had decided on the alliance; Berthier was welcomed as proxy in Vienna, and Court and city gave themselves up to congenial festivities.

Napoleon was now forty-one: Marie Louise an attractive blonde of eighteen, with all the style and poise of her upbringing. She had a rather sensual face with full lips and slanting blue eyes; brought up in Vienna, she loved good food and gaiety and she was an amateur artist. She was also methodical; unlike Josephine,

OPPOSITE ABOVE The Rue de Rivoli, showing the Italianate arcades introduced by Napoleon.

OPPOSITE BELOW The bronze horses which Napoleon took back to France with him from St Mark's, Venice to adorn the Austerlitz Arch.

careful about money; a high-bred Hapsburg royalty, but limited, easy-going and easily led. She should have arrived in Paris on 27 March, but Napoleon rushed to meet her, and bedded her at once, very successfully, at Compiègne. His Court took on a new gaiety and the Emperor learned the new and fashionable waltz. In May, three weeks after their wedding, Napoleon took his young Empress to the former Austrian Netherlands, to show the people, including the numerous Catholics shocked by his treatment of the Pope, that Belgium was now irrevocably French.

At this juncture, Louis, King of Holland, under pressure from powerful commercial interests who detested the boycott of trade with England, was impelled to side with his subjects against the Emperor; he refused to admit French troops to Breda and Bergen-op-Zoom, and then abdicated. In May 1810 Napoleon wrote to him in fury, 'I've long known that you want to make trouble in Holland, and by your follies cause the ruin of that country. Don't write me any more of your platitudes, you've been repeating them for three years. This is the last letter I will ever write to you in my life.' Holland had to be annexed into the Empire, an action that terrified banking interests all over Europe; this and the state visit to Antwerp were not a promising background for the overtures Napoleon was now making to the English.

It still seemed essential to maintain the blockade; the over-riding strategy that alone might bring England down, and the Empire's main strategic objective now to be reinforced from Sweden in the continuing war. When, in August, Charles XIII, the last of the Vasas, adopted Bernadotte, now Prince of Pontecorvo, as his successor, and the Swedes elected him heir apparent, it had been a chance decision, made mainly to keep a Danish candidate out. In spite of Bernadotte's record, Napoleon consented, hoping to keep Sweden in line. All was in vain. On the last day of 1810, the Tsar Alexander, under pressure from Russian commercial interests, promulgated a Ukase commanding free trade for all neutrals coming to Russian ports. They came loaded up with English and colonial goods, and Riga became the biggest gap in Napoleon's grand design.

When, therefore, on 19 March 1811, after a hard delivery, Marie Louise bore Napoleon a son, and the thunder of 101 guns greeted the occasion, the future was not as propitious as it looked for the beautiful child – 'l'Aiglon' – 'the Eaglet' – one of the more tragic minor figures in European history. Yet he symbolized so much: through his father, the historic French ambition to

139

An engraving of Hortense,
Queen of Holland and
daughter of Josephine,
by Adlard.

dominate Europe; through his mother, the ancient Hapsburg
claims to the supreme authority of the old Holy Roman Empire.
It was not for nothing that he was created King of Rome.

That summer, relations with the Russians were getting worse.
The introduction of that modern institution, the *Code Civil*, and
the toleration of Jews even in a truncated Grand Duchy of
Warsaw, roused suspicion and fear in Russia. If the detested
Poles got on their feet, Polish serfs were emancipated and equality
allowed before the law, the iron despotism of the Tsars, which
alone could sustain their gigantic sprawling society, would be
undermined. The Russian ambassador protested in Paris, and
Napoleon made one of his calculated tirades: 'Even though your
armies were to camp on the heights of Montmartre, I should not
yield an inch of Warsaw. You know that I have 800,000 men.'
Caulaincourt, the French ambassador to Russia, warned Napoleon
of the danger, but his warnings were disregarded; one battle,

Louis, her husband, who was one of Napoleon's brothers and was made King of Holland by him.

said the Emperor, would again dispose of Alexander, a poor character, and irresolute. But Alexander Pávlovich had already made up his mind on how to deal with Napoleon. 'The system', he wrote to the King of Prussia in May 1811, 'which has made Wellington victorious in Spain, and exhausted the French armies, is what I intend to follow – avoid pitched battles, and organize long lines of communication for retreat leading to entrenched camps.'

The Tsar had good reason to keep his eyes on Spain. All through the years that had seen the defeat of Austria, the Hapsburg marriage and the apparently unprecedented extent and power of Napoleon's empire, the Spanish war had been going on; and it was not going well for the French.

In April 1809, Sir Arthur Wellesley, this time in full command, had again arrived in Portugal with twenty-five thousand men,

141

The 'lines' of Torres Vedras before which Masséna was forced to retreat in the autumn of 1810.

and been received in what the English called 'Black Horse Square' in Lisbon by the rejoicing populace, 'groups dancing to castanets and drums, plump ladies in painted litters or Sedan chairs . . . short handsome gentlemen in tricorne hats . . . peasants in long straw cloaks, white shirts, blue drawers and black shovel hats'. The French command had now been divided, with Soult and the Army of Portugal almost independent in the south; pay had long been in arrears and the two hundred thousand men tied up in Spain had been living as best they could off a country seething with hatred.

Wellesley was just the dogged and cautious commander for a

142

long extended and gruelling war, well experienced in India of
the difficulties of supply in hard country. He had soon liberated
Oporto and struck deep into Spain, forcing the French to concentrate against him when Napoleon wanted all the men he
could get for the Austrian campaign, still in the balance until
Wagram; and at the end of July he had held the field at the
terrible battle of Talavera, south-west of Madrid, against forty
thousand of the French, a victory for which Wellesley had been
created Viscount Wellington. The French now had to drive him
back to his prepared position on the double 'lines' of Torres
Vedras, a range of forts and strong-points across the high country

The storming of Badajoz by Wellington's troops in
March 1812. Some of Napoleon's troops had been
withdrawn to prepare for the invasion of Russia, and the
French suffered a crushing defeat.

about twenty miles north of Cintra and Lisbon between the sea and the Tagus estuary. After Wagram, Napoleon had sent Masséna with more massive forces to drive Wellington to his ships; but at Busaco Masséna had failed before the English fire-power, and 1810 had opened with the French at the end of a line of difficult communications; the Spanish regulars and guerrillas better organized; and the British and Portuguese at bay but supplied by sea. All through that year, while Napoleon had made his great dynastic marriage to consolidate a European empire, this Spanish deadlock had gone on: then, on 5 March 1811, Masséna, his supplies failing, and under cover of fog, had retreated towards Coimbra and the Mondego valley. But Wellington and the Portuguese had at once followed him and forced him east into Spain, with great loss through difficult and hostile country. The French had suffered and committed appalling atrocities and they had lost nearly all Portugal.

That summer, when Napoleon's relations with Russia had been worsening, Wellington had launched a second offensive to break into Spain against the French-held fortresses of Ciudad Rodrigo guarding Salamanca and their communications with France, and Badajoz on the Guadiana, guarding southern central Spain and Andalusia. In the north, in May, Napoleon had forced Masséna to attack to relieve the French garrison still at Almeida in Portugal west of Salamanca, but he had been defeated at Fuentes de Onoro west of Ciudad Rodrigo. Though the garrison had broken out, Masséna had been contemptuously relieved of his command and replaced by Marmont, Duke of Ragusa.

In the south, too, that month, the British and their allies had defeated Soult at Albuera and forced him to retire on Seville. Wellington had then taken command, and by January 1812 his armies had stormed Ciudad Rodrigo and, by March, Badajoz. The key fortresses defending Spain had been lost. Then in July, at the height of Napoleon's preparations to invade Russia, the French were defeated in the great battle at Salamanca and in August Wellington and his allies briefly liberated Madrid. The long Spanish war would be drawing most heavily on French resources just when Napoleon was launched on his greatest and most disastrous gamble, the Russian campaign of 1812. The brittle greatness was cracking up.

7 The Nemesis of Power 1812-14

He could not stop what was going on before him and
around him and was supposed to be directed by him and
depend on him and ... the affair, for the first time,
seemed unnecessary and horrible.

TOLSTOI   *War and Peace*

CONTRARY TO WIDESPREAD OPINION, Napoleon never wanted to invade Russia. He was not driven by an insatiable lust for war or a romantic wish to conquer Moscow, *'la capitale asiatique de ce grand empire, la ville sacrée des peuples d'Alexandre, Moscou avec ses innombrables églises en forme de pagodas chinoises'* ('the Asiatic capital of this great empire, the holy city of the peoples of Alexander, Moscow with her innumerable churches looking like Chinese pagodas'). He was driven by the logic of the situation in which he was entrapped. It was essential to bring back the Russians into the *blocus continental* against England, and he intended, as at Friedland, to catch and break their armies and so bring the Tsar to terms.

As early as the autumn of 1811, the colossal enterprise had begun, and that December, he had sent for a full account of Charles XIII of Sweden's campaigns in Russia. By May 1812, he had concentrated six hundred thousand men in Poland on the Vistula and on 22 June he issued a typical proclamation: 'Soldiers! The Second Polish War has begun! Russia has broken all her promises. ... Russia is drawn to her Fate.' But Napoleon and his armies were being drawn to theirs.

The Emperor had made his headquarters on the Baltic; first at Danzig, then at Königsberg. The principal problem was not manpower – he could draw on the resources of a vast empire; indeed, although politically precarious, it made a good war map; but, as he wrote, 'In this kind of country bread is what matters most.' He did not, it seems, at first reckon on a long war and thought that he could repeat the successes of Austerlitz and Friedland, quickly destroy the Russian armies and force the Tsar, whom he still felt he could dominate, to make peace. Obviously any long-term occupation in Russia would be impracticable, but one good battle would dispose of all.

The nucleus and striking force of the immense polyglot armies was the Imperial Guard. So long as it remained intact, it could sheer through anything that even the Russians could set against it. The rest of the army was less efficient – the Poles were ardent, and most of the young French conscripts keen if inexperienced, but few Germans, Italians, Czechs or Hungarians can have been enthusiastic save for plunder.

On 25 June Napoleon crossed the Niemen, making for Vilna with 450,000 men. 'I have come, once and for all', he said, 'to deal with the colossus of the barbarian north.' In fact, apart from the Guard, Napoleon's own expedition was more like the 'bar-

barian' composite armies of Xerxes than the relatively compact
forces he had manœuvred and controlled with such brilliance in
his earlier battles. And if his armies were unwieldy, Napoleon
was not physically quite the man he had been: he now suffered
from a bladder inflammation and piles, disabilities very in-
convenient for one long in the saddle; he had put on weight, and
his clear-cut predatory profile had coarsened with middle age.
He had long driven himself too hard, and incessant crowding
experiences and responsibilities difficult to imagine must have
taken their toll. Long accustomed to autocracy, speaking by
convention the high-flown language of empire, he was now even
more impulsive and domineering; yet, as over Spain, the note of
exasperation would increase. The inefficiency of the huge army
made him furious: by September, when they were well into
Russia, he would remark 'I've been commanding French armies
for twenty years and I've never seen the military administration
so useless.'

The Russians could at first mobilize no more than 160,000
men, but they had already gained two, advantages. In April
Bernadotte, now Charles John, Crown Prince of Sweden and
deputy for the aged Charles XIII, had been impelled by the
merchants and investors who suffered from the blockade to go
over to the Tsar, his price a free hand against Denmark and
Norway. Here was a diplomatic revolution on the Baltic caused
in part by Napoleon's occupation of Swedish Pomerania to
impose the blockade, and it followed the Russian decision to
make peace with England. In the south, too, the Turks, after ·the
long campaign in which Kutúzov had won success and experience,
had come to terms at Bucharest. Russia was now at peace with
both her traditional enemies.

As usual, the Russian arrangements of command were un-
satisfactory. The Tsar remained nominally in control, but he was
always under changing influences and his Prussian adviser Phull,
Barclay de Tolly and Bagration were at odds. Yet had the armies
been better organized, they might have stood, fought and been
overwhelmed: their inefficiency as well as their endurance saved
them. There was no unified command until August, when, after
Smolensk had fallen, Kutúzov was at last appointed Commander-
in-Chief.

Napoleon had struck due east into Lithuania to bring the
Russians to battle at Vilna, capture massive supplies and threaten
both St Petersburg and Moscow. But he found most of the place

Eugène de Beauharnais,
Napoleon's stepson.
Napoleon had great
faith in him.

burned out and the depots destroyed: Russians are good at this. Characteristically, too, the Poles now claimed that he should now revive the huge old kingdom of Poland and Lithuania and sulked when, under obligations to Austria, Napoleon refused.

The failure to catch the Russian armies and the disappointment at Vilna proved demoralizing, and there were so many desertions that Murat, Berthier and Eugène, the three commanders closest to him, urged Napoleon to call the campaign off. And so he did for two days; then, taunting them with being too soft for war, he went on with it. What sort of reception would he get in Germany or France if he returned under a cloud of defeat?

The army now advanced deep into Russia itself, making for Smolensk on the Dnieper on the road to Moscow; and it was deemed that the Russians must stand there. August is a hot month in Russia, and the march on Moscow, most notorious for its retreat through intense cold, was begun in oppressive heat. Through the vast monotonous country the army trudged on to Smolensk, where on 17 August they failed to envelop the Russian army outside it or even the Russians in it; moreover, after a bombardment, vividly evoked by Tolstoi, they were again con-

150

An engraving after Saint-Aubin's drawing of Prince Michael Kutúzov.

fronted with a burned-out city. Three days after, Kutúzov took over his command.

The invaders were now about half way to Moscow from the frontier and Napoleon pushed on. At Dorogobuzh the dust and heat were atrocious, desertions and sickness further thinned the army, and the horses were in a bad way. Then at Borodino, on the Moskva, the Russians stood to fight. Kutúzov had not wanted to, but he had to yield to patriotic feeling – nor did the event turn out badly for the Russians; they suffered frightful casualties and the French held the field, but there were plenty more Russians and no reinforcement for the impious invaders. The essential thing was to kill them, and the Russians knew how to do it.

On 1 September at Borodino Napoleon fought what he would describe as the 'most terrible of all my battles': the French casualties were thirty thousand, including over forty generals; the Russians over fifty thousand. It was a slaughter surpassing that of Eylau. Napoleon had just had the news of the resounding defeat of Marmont's army on 22 July in Spain, where the French, over-extended to cut off the British retirement on Ciudad Rodrigo, had been trapped south of Salamanca and the river Tormes when

The battle of Borodino, fought in September 1812: Lejeune's painting. Napoleon thought it 'the most terrible of all my battles. ... The French showed themselves worthy of victory, and the Russians worthy of being invincible.'

Wellington's right wing had emerged to fall upon them from the Arapile hills. They had suffered fourteen thousand casualties, and on 12 August Wellington had entered Madrid. He had now proved himself not simply a master of defensive warfare, but formidable on the offensive as well.

To add to his difficulties, the Emperor also had a thick and feverish cold, and did not show his usual mastery; but he played safe and did not throw in the Guard; 'The last reserves', he said, 'are not risked eight hundred leagues from France.' The Russians had drawn off, but they were not annihilated and Kutúzov remained in the offing. Other great armies were being organized.

Napoleon was surprised to find Moscow in the middle of a sandy forested plain, hard going for the surviving horses and the exhausted army. And the expected deputation of Boyars bearing bread, salt and the civic keys did not arrive; when the invaders entered the sprawling city it was almost deserted in a sinister, dusty silence. That very night the fires began: in the dry September weather the wooden houses burned like matchwood, for the governor, Count Rostopchin, had removed what rudimentary fire-fighting devices there were. Napoleon described the scene as 'literally an ocean of fire'; great areas of Moscow went up in flame and smoke, and only about a quarter of the place was left. The French tried to save the buildings that looked promising for loot and the massive buildings of the Kremlin survived, but the Asian ruthlessness of the gesture appalled them. It had not been so in Vienna, Rome or Berlin.

Still hoping for a settlement, Napoleon wrote to the Tsar making the worst of it. 'The beautiful and superb city of Moscow no longer exists. . . . It is impossible that you can have sanctioned this. I have made war on you without animosity. . . . If your Majesty retains any of your former sentiments towards me, you will take this letter in good part.' It was odd that Napoleon still stood by the false civilities, the exchange of furs and Sèvres: naturally the letter was left unanswered.

Yet in the strange hope that Alexander would – or could – come to terms, Napoleon remained a whole month losing precious time in the ruined city. The wily Kutúzov lulled him by an informal truce, and Cossack officers were instructed to fraternize with the French and dwell upon the demoralization and disorganization of Russia and on the Russian people's wish for peace. In fact, they were resolved with the same resolution as would defy Hitler, and at any cost, to make the foreigners, as Stalin would

Cossacks pursuing the retreating French, by J. A. Klein.

put it, 'take their pig snouts out of' their 'garden'. And when, on 16 October, the Emperor offered Kutúzov peace, his overture was rejected at once.

In the continental Russian fall, as in North America, there is a brief deceptive warmth; 'better', said Napoleon, 'than at Fontaine-bleau', and that year better than usual. Yet to winter in ruined Moscow was impossible, nor could communications with the west be kept secure. By the end of the month, mainly in view of reports of conspiracy in Paris, Napoleon had resolved to do what he had done in Egypt and desert his army. He would not in fact do so until he had saved part of it at the Berezina, but he knew that he would have to get back to Paris. Already from Moscow he had ordered another conscription of 140,000 young men.

The first snow of the winter fell on 15 October. On the 19th, with 100,000 men out of the original 450,000, the Emperor moved out of Moscow, in exasperation leaving engineers detailed to blow up the Kremlin – an order fortunately not carried out. The long, slow columns were now weighed down with plunder, with sick

155

and wounded, with supplies and fodder; if the remaining horses perished, the cavalry could not fend off the Cossacks. The army had never been equipped for cold; only the Emperor's own horses were shod for ice and that on the insistence of Caulaincourt who, as a former ambassador, knew the country. Napoleon resolved to return by the direct but devastated route through Smolensk. 'The Guard', he had ordered, 'will bivouac in a square round the Emperor': 'We are returning', he said, 'to Poland where I will

BELOW Ferdinand Boissard's painting conveys the horror of the retreat from Moscow in the bitterly cold Russian winter.

156

take up good winter quarters and I hope that Alexander will make peace.' But the Russians soon started to harry the columns; once, after a battle at Malojaroslavetz which cost the French heavy casualties, the Cossacks nearly captured Napoleon himself, but were diverted to plunder some supply carts. The French were now being forced along the worst ravaged country and still some two hundred miles from Smolensk when at the end of October, the real cold struck. Napoleon now sometimes marched on foot; it was warmer than riding.

By 6 November snow and deep frost had fully set in: stragglers began to fall out or beg refuge in Russian huts, where they were lured in and had their throats cut: an English observer with Kutúsov saw 'sixty dying naked men, whose necks were laid upon a felled tree while Russian men and women with large faggot-sticks, singing in chorus and hopping round, with repeated blows struck out their brains'. The wolves, their high sinister ululation haunting the nights, also moved in for their kill. Three days later, the French were at ruined Smolensk, where Napoleon rested for three days, then blew up what remained of the fortifications, and the horrible trek began again, the Emperor, in a fur cap, marching in the middle of the Guard. Nearly all the horses were now dead; they had perished on the slippery ice or through the awful cold. Fresh Russian armies were now closing in from north and south and Napoleon's caution in withholding the Guard at Borodino was vindicated, for at Krasnoi, when Kutúzov barred the way, he ordered them to attack. 'It is certain', writes Markham, 'that without them Napoleon would never have returned from Russia.' Davydov, the Russian partisan leader, describes how 'The guard with Napoleon passed through our Cossacks like a hundred gun ship through a fishing fleet.' The rearguard under Ney held off the enemy, but out of eight thousand of them only eight hundred survived.

It was not until the 25th that the army arrived at the Berezina west of Minsk, a town already taken by the Russians, with their fighting strength even further diminished and with only 250 guns. The three Russian armies numbered nearly 150,000 men and the Berezina was not yet frozen hard; it was in flood with jostling ice floes. The bridges had been destroyed, the Russians already held the bank opposite and so desperate appeared the situation that it seemed that Napoleon must capitulate. But the French had luck: peasants, wanting to get rid of them, had given it away that at Studienka the river was only a hundred yards wide and six

The Campaigns
of Poland and Russia
1807 and 1812

Scale 0   50   100 miles

N

ESTONIA

LIVONIA

BALTIC SEA

COURLAND

Riga

R. Dvina

Jacobstadt

KOVNO

Memel

Shavli

Rossieny

Tauroggen

Keidany

Vilkomir

Sventsian

Gulf of
Danzig

Tilsit

Kovno

R. Vilia

Königsberg

R. Pregel

Insterburg

Neustadt

Danzig

Eylau

Friedland

Stallupohen

Piloni

Vilna

Elbing

R. Alle

Gumbinnen

Vilkovischi

Ponarskaia

Marienburg

To Stettin

Allenstein

Ochmiana

LITHUANIA

Marienwerder

Lida

To Posen

EAST PRUSSIA

Grodno

R. Niemen

Thorn

Biezun

Vilkavischi

R. Vistula

R. Ukra

Pultusk

R. Narew

Bialystock

Slonim

WARSAW

R. Bug

Brest-Litovsk

GRAND DUCHY OF
WARSAW

Lublin

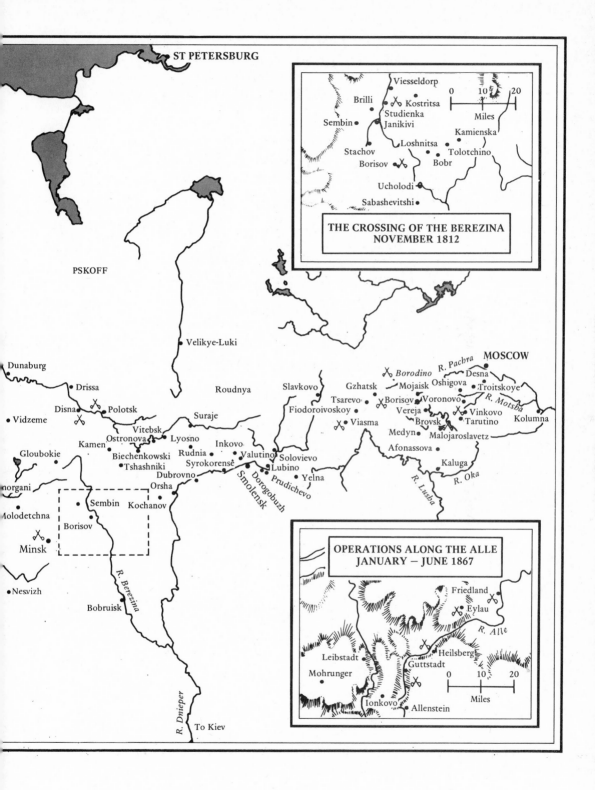

ST PETERSBURG

PSKOFF

Velikye-Luki

Dunaburg

Drissa

Disna

Polotsk

Vidzeme

Roudnya

Suraje

Slavkovo

Kamen

Ostronova

Vitebsk

Lyosno

Inkovo

Gloubokie

Biechenkowski

Tshashniki

Rudnia

Syrokorense

Valutino

Soloviev

Lubino

morgani

Dubrovno

Orsha

Dorogobuzh

Prudichevo

Yelna

Molodetchna

Sembin

Kochanov

Borisov

Minsk

Nesvizh

Bobruisk

R. Berezina

R. Dnieper

To Kiev

Smolensk

MOSCOW

Borodino

R. Pachra

Desna

Gzhatsk

Mojaisk

Oshigova

Troitskoye

Tsarevo

Borisov

Voronovo

R. Motsha

Fiodoroivoskoy

Vereja

Vinkovo

Kolumna

Viasma

Brovsk

Tarutino

Medyn

Malojaroslavetz

Afonassova

Kaluga

R. Oka

R. Lusha

THE CROSSING OF THE BEREZINA
NOVEMBER 1812

Viesseldorp

Brilli

Kostritsa

Studienka

Sembin

Janikivi

Loshnitsa

Kamienska

0   10   20

Miles

Stachov

Tolotchino

Borisov

Bobr

Ucholodi

Sabashevitshi

OPERATIONS ALONG THE ALLE
JANUARY – JUNE 1867

Friedland

Eylau

R. Alle

Heilsberg

Leibstadt

Guttstadt

Mohrunger

0   10   20

Miles

Ionkovo

Allenstein

feet deep. Here was the answer: 'I have played the Emperor long enough', said Napoleon, 'It is time I played the general.' With a brilliant tactical virtuosity, he feinted as though to cross south of the village so that the Russians conformed, but in fact within twenty-four hours, his carpenters and engineers constructed a bridge over this relatively shallow reach. The infantry crossed first, in time to shoot it out with the returning Russians in front, and though men were drowned and trampled into the ice, by the time the pursuing Russians from the east arrived, most of the army and its guns were across. The whole operation had taken only two days.

On 6 December, having squared the marshals by appealing to their interests in preserving his regime, Napoleon left the army for Paris, leaving Murat in command. On 5 November Napoleon had been informed of an attempted *coup* in Paris by a crazy republican general, Malet, who had proclaimed the Emperor's death, and briefly mastered the city. The event had, in fact, proved farcical; but Napoleon had been horrified that no one had thought of proclaiming the King of Rome. The Emperor travelled incognito, at first by sledge, with Caulaincourt and Roustam in attendance. There was one asset left – the terror of his name – and he intended to mobilize the whole resources of France. Meanwhile, the *Bulletin to the Army* published ten days later was good political warfare: far from minimizing the catastrophe, Napoleon dramatized it, putting in the full details of the *débâcle* and of the gallantry of the fighting retreat; the disaster was attributed not to the Russians but to the climate. Significantly, it ended 'The health of his Majesty has never been better.' He had still to be reckoned with.

He made for Dresden, and by 18 December he was in the Tuileries. Two days later he admitted to the Senate, with an understatement surpassing that of the *Bulletin*, 'My army has had some losses, but it was due to the premature rigour of the climate.' He ordered yet another massive call-up from the whole Empire. If he could keep France behind him in defence of the 'natural' frontiers of the Rhine, the Alps and the Pyrenees secured by the Revolution, he might yet negotiate from strength.

As 1813 dawned, Napoleon was not without assets. The Austrians were terrified of Russia, afraid of revolution in Germany, afraid of Prussian nationalism. Even Metternich, whose Rhineland estates had been overrun, wanted to keep Napoleon, if he could

ABOVE The little King of Rome, 'the hope of the French'.

BELOW An anonymous water-colour illustrating a fashionable gathering at the Louvre in 1801.

tame him in the interests of a general settlement and a restoration of the balance of power, for which the English had always been fighting. Such a settlement, had Napoleon willed it, would have been hard to sell to the French people had it meant giving up Belgium, though some compromise might even here have been accepted. But Napoleon still thought he could win. With vast conscript armies mobilized, he might still hope to defeat the Russians and Prussians, while Austria remained nominally neutral.

The Russians were already in Prussia, where at the end of December the Prussian General Yorck had gone over to them. And the Prussians were mobilizing; Napoleon wrote to Eugène, now Commander-in-Chief there, 'At the least insult in a . . . . town or village, burn it. Do this in Berlin if they misbehave.' On 28 March Frederick William II declared war and, at once, Napoleon concentrated a great army at Mainz. In May, at Lutzen south of Leipzig in the heart of north and central Germany, Napoleon personally led a cavalry charge in a victorious battle. He directed his propaganda mainly against the Russians: 'We will throw back these barbarians into their icy deserts, scene of slavery and corruption. You have deserved well of European civilization, soldiers of Italy, France, Germany, I thank you!' He was appealing to the young conscripts, who had fought hard but without enough good officers; and only the lack of cavalry had prevented Napoleon from following up his success. So again at Bautzen, east of Dresden, he drove the Russians beyond the Oder, but did not annihilate his opponents. He still hoped that the Austrians would back him, and made an armistice at Pleiswitz which led to a peace conference at Prague. But by now the Austrian game was becoming clearer – 'They want to make a golden bridge', he complained, 'for Alexander.' They were betraying the alliance and 'by pretending to mediate wanted to take all'.

Meanwhile, the Spanish disaster was mounting to its climax. In June Wellington had won his greatest strategic victory at Vittoria in northern Spain when, having advanced through mountainous country to the west of the route from Madrid to France, he had swung east and defeated Jourdan's army making north, and captured a fantastic quantity of guns and loot, including the French Marshal's baton, adorned with thirty-two golden eagles. King Joseph had barely escaped. And Wellington had here made his famous and often misrepresented remark contrasting his own volunteer army with the conscript French: 'The conscription

OPPOSITE A portrait of Metternich after Lawrence. He said of Napoleon: 'In whatever time he had appeared he would have played a prominent part.'

162

Tarjarat's watercolour of the battle of Moscow. The Russian strategy of
retreat took Napoleon completely by surprise, unplanned though it was.

calls forth a share of every class . . . but our friends, I may say in this room, are the very scum of the earth. . . . You can hardly conceive such a set brought together, and it is really wonderful that we should have made them such fine fellows as they are.' And again, we were 'never equal in numbers, but they [the French] cannot stand us now at all'. Wellington had been created a marquess and promoted Field Marshal: 'in the corridors of Central European power, the statesmen felt marvellously strengthened to resist Napoleon.'

'The miseries of Spain', wrote the Emperor, 'are as great as they are absurd.' Joseph had been *de trop* and the generals incompetent: 'In the last analysis', he confessed, 'I blame myself.' Worst of all, had he known it, on 15 June the English had signed treaties with Russia and Prussia that they would not make any separate peace, and again heavily subsidized both powers.

On 26 June at the elegant Marcolini Palace at Dresden, then one of the most attractive of German cities, Napoleon received Metternich, and was staggered at the Austrian demands. They were nothing less than the break-up of the French Empire – the cession of Illyria and northern Italy to Austria, of most of Poland to the Russians and the dissolution of the Confederation of the Rhine. Metternich indicated that if he did not accept them, Austria would declare war. Napoleon in rage threw his hat across the room – and Metternich left it there: the Emperor now had either to abandon his Empire or to appear as the public enemy of Europe. On 12 August the Austrians entered the war and he had the three great continental powers as well as England all against him at once. Bernadotte was now also in the field against him and the Spanish disaster still tied up large armies in Spain.

By the autumn of 1813 Napoleon again had a big army in Germany, including forty thousand cavalry and ample artillery; but the Allies had even greater manpower. After failing to defeat the converging Allies in detail from Dresden, he fell back on Leipzig, but with only 160,000 men against the Allies' 300,000. An Austrian army under Schwarzenberg, the supreme commander of the Allies, was emerging from the Erzgirbirge massif of Bohemia – that strategic key to central Europe; a Prussian army under Blücher was converging south. Leipzig was the most monstrous of all the Emperor's battles – worse in scale even than Borodino, with massed artillery inflicting appalling carnage on relatively level terrain. It lasted three days, the middle one a truce of exhaustion, and has been called the 'Battle of the Nations'

The Marcolini Palace at Dresden where Napoleon received Metternich: an early twentieth-century photograph.

or a 'soldiers' battle', which means one in which more soldiers are killed than usual. The French lost forty thousand casualties and twenty thousand prisoners, taken because, during the retreat, the one bridge over the Elster was destroyed too soon. The Allies lost at least fifty-four thousand, but it was the first great battle with Napoleon in full command in which he suffered total defeat, and it was the end of Napoleon's Empire. He got out through the Thuringer Wald down to Hanau east of Frankfurt, where he broke through Allied resistance and regrouped at Mainz; but apart from the big garrisons in north Germany, he now had no more than sixty thousand men.

166

By November 1814 he was again back in Paris. All did not even then seem lost, for a coalition is a coalition, and the Allies had little relish for tackling the tiger on his home ground. It was indicated semi-officially that France might still retain her 'natural frontiers'; but Napoleon, who hoped still to rout his enemies, refused these favourable terms — which were probably insincere. Then, on 4 December, the Allies stepped up their political warfare: the Declaration of Frankfurt was not indeed precise, but it guaranteed more territories to the French than France had ever had under her kings. As they were meant to do, the civilian French Legislature took the bait, so that Napoleon declared that

167

Staffordshire Gazette Office,

THURSDAY NIGHT, NINE O'CLOCK.

Bonaparte defeated in Person! 20 Generals Killed or Prisoners! The King of Saxony and all his Court taken Prisoners! LEIPSIC taken by Storm! The Total Loss of the French Army, 82,000 Men and 180 Pieces of Cannon!

BULLETIN.

"Foreign Office, Nov. 3, 1813.

" DISPATCHES were this morning received by Viscount Castlereagh, from Lieut. General Sir Charles Stewart, dated Leipsic, October 19, giving the details of a complete and signal victory gained by the whole of the Combined Armies of Bohemia, Silesia, and the North of Germany, over Bonaparte, in the neighbourhood of Leipsic, on the 18th and 19th.

" One hundred pieces of cannon, sixty thousand killed, wounded, and prisoners; the whole of the Saxon army, and the Bavarian and Wurtemberg troops, consisting of cavalry, artillery and infantry; many Generals, among whom are Regnier, Valary, Brune, Bertrand, and Lauriston, are stated to be the fruits of this glorious day.

" On the morning of the 19th, Leipsic was taken by storm, with the King of Saxony, and all his Court, the garrison, and rear-guard of the French army, and 30,000 wounded.—Bonaparte narrowly escaped.—He fled from Leipsic at nine o'clock; the Allies entering at eleven; the French Army completely routed, and endeavouring to escape in all directions.

" Before the bearer of the Dispatches left the neighbourhood of Leipsic, 35,000 prisoners had been brought in, and the Official Bulletin of Berlin of the 21st states, 180 pieces of cannon to have been taken. Macdonald and Souham also prisoners.

" On the 16th, General Blucher had attacked the 4th, 6th, and 7th corps of the French Army on the north side of Leipsic—stormed a range of batteries—took forty pieces of cannon—one eagle—many caissons—and the enemy lost Twelve Thousand killed and wounded.

Dresden is reported to have been entered on the 18th.

The Royal Family of Saxony was taken in a charge headed by the Crown Prince.

FIRST BATTLE, AND DEFEAT OF THE FRENCH!!

After a hard and sanguinary action, which continued for some hours, Ney was defeated, with the loss of 12,000 men.

SECOND BATTLE!

This battle, fought on the same day as the first, was equally well contested and bloody. But at length Bonaparte succeeded in breaking through the centre of the Prince of Schwartzenberg's army, by bringing up the whole of his cavalry, under Murat. The Allies then brought up their reserve, and drove Bonaparte back upon the point he occupied before he pierced the Prince of Schwartzenberg's centre. The battle terminated at night, and both armies remained in sight of each other, without either having gained any material advantage. On the 17th, they prepared for the more important Battle that was to take place next day.

THE THIRD BATTLE, AND DEFEAT BATTLE OF BONAPARTE:

By the 18th, the Allies having collected and concentrated their forces under the Crown Prince and Blucher, and the Prince of Schwartzenberg, attacked Bonaparte in all his positions. He fought with the determination, the desperation, that a man may be supposed to have, who feels that his Crown perhaps depends upon the issue of the conflict. But his obstinacy, his talents, his skill, were unavailing. He was defeated with the loss of about 40,000 men, and nearly 200 pieces of cannon.

Without giving the enemy a day's respite, the Allies advanced to Leipsic the day after the glorious victory, and after a most bloody resistance, took it by storm, with 30,000 prisoners, and a great number of cannon, ammunition waggons, &c &c. That, in four days, Bonaparte's army was reduced one-half, a more rapid and enormous loss than he sustained in the same space of time, even in his calamitous campaign in Russia.

Loss on the 16th, by NEY 12,000
On the 18th, by BONAPARTE in person 40,000
On the 19th, in the Storming of Leipsic 30,000

TOTAL 82,000

Driven from Leipsic, Bonaparte attempted to retreat by Erfurt, the direct road to the Rhine. He failed.—the road was already occupied by his conquerors. His retreat to Erfurt was cut off. Bonaparte, with the wreck and remnant of his Army, took the road toward Brunswick, thus removing further from his resources and his reinforcements. The Allies were in pursuit of him, and he is destined, we trust, to experience fresh disasters and defeat. May we now retort upon him his own words, and say, ' Surely the Finger of Providence is here.!

Of the Officers that fell on either side we have no detailed account. Macdonald, Souham, and Poniatowski, were made prisoners. Regnier, Lauriston, Bertrand, Valary, and Brune, killed. The King of Saxony has been rescued from the Tyrant's yoke, with all his Court.

All the Saxons and Bavarians, and Wurtemburg troops came over to the Allies. Bonaparte narrowly escaped, he fled from Leipsic two hours only before the Allies entered it.

The Park and Tower guns were fired at eleven o'clock. The bells are Ringing, and Illuminations, we suppose, will follow.

Smith, Printer, Newcastle.

it was himself, not they, who represented France. In fact, by the end of 1813 the English had categorically stated that they would sign no peace without the liberation of Holland and the surrender of Antwerp, and when in February 1814, another conference would be held at Châtillon-sur-Seine, the Allied terms would be less attractive.

Meanwhile, Napoleon's government was heading for bank-ruptcy; the last reserves, including all but ten million of his gigantic personal hoard of seventy-five million francs, had been thrown in. The new conscription was widely evaded and taxation was savagely increased. Ever since Leipzig, when the Saxons had defected and turned their guns on the French, the components of the Empire had been breaking up. Jerome's Westphalian kingdom collapsed at once; in January Holland revolted; Baden, Bavaria, Württemburg and the rest of the Confederation turned against the French. In February Murat in Naples, instigated by Caroline, declared war on Napoleon.

Napoleon now shrewdly played on the fears of the Parisians – at all cost the Cossacks must be stopped; he at once sent the Pope

ABOVE Jerome Bonaparte, the longest-lived brother of Napoleon, and King of Westphalia. The portrait is after Kinson.
OPPOSITE An English newsbill – the *Staffordshire Gazette* announcing the defeat of Napoleon at the battle of Leipzig in 1813.

back to Rome and Fernando VII from his luxurious captivity back to Spain. He appointed Marie Louise as Regent and, unwisely, ex-King Joseph as Lieutenant of the Realm. But his fixed idea was to save his dynasty for his son: he would rather see him killed, he said, than brought up as an Austrian Prince in Vienna – in fact, his fate. But Napoleon's diplomacy had only been playing for time; he had started as a soldier and adventurer and he would end as one. On 25 January 1814 he parted from Marie Louise and the boy. He would never see them again.

His final campaign was a triumph of virtuosity, much admired by experts in the military art. His strategy was to make Paris a fortress, then strike at the flanks and communications of the invaders as they converged on it and got further from base. And had Paris held out, the strategy might well have worked; but Paris was defeatist, and Talleyrand, on Napoleon's return, had remarked 'Don't bother me with your Emperor – he's finished. . . . I mean that he's a man ready to hide under the bed.' Talleyrand was now resolved to be the mediator who arranged a Bourbon restoration. Napoleon played all his tricks of propaganda – an engraving of the little King of Rome praying the Almighty for his father's victory was widely popular; the young conscripts – known as 'Marie Louises' from their appearance and from being summoned under her Regency, were harangued, and often with effect, but some could hardly load a musket. The consensus of bourgeois and military interest was breaking up; the Bourse slumped; the despotic rule of Napoleon had cowed the bureaucracy and undermined initiative and the sense of responsibility. The Parisians did not want their city to be made another Moscow, though Napoleon would have been capable of making it one. In contrast to the spirit of 1870-1 and in conformity with that of 1940, there was no civilian resistance; the defending troops, hopelessly outnumbered, would fight a last action in Montmartre, then capitulate. Since the whole strategy turned on Paris's holding out, the campaign was foredoomed.

Wellington, meanwhile, after the frustrating autumn and winter campaign of 1812 to force the Pyrenees against Soult, Duke of Dalmatia, nicknamed by the British 'the Duke of Damnation', had defeated his counter-offensive in late July 1813, at Sorauren. Then on 31 August, San Sebastian had been captured, and by 7 October the Anglo-Spanish-Portuguese armies had crossed the estuary of the Bidassoa into France. Early in November they had

Marshal Soult, 'the Duke of Damnation', one of Napoleon's most competent generals, painted by an unknown artist.

crossed the Nivelle and by December they were threatening the main French base at Bayonne. The first invasion had come from the south.

Then in January 1814, Blücher had invaded France from the Rhineland. Following the Allies' plan to converge on Paris, the Prussians and Russians along the Marne, the Austrians along the Seine, the campaign was fought out in the historic area in the modern departments of Marne and Seine-et-Marne. It was very rapid: Napoleon fought six battles in nine days, and they co-incided with the negotiations at Châtillon. In fact, politically, Napoleon's exploits did not pay off, for they made him refuse good terms in the hope of better.

On 29 January he defeated Blücher at Brienne near the Aube – the scene of his own early training. On 1 February he was worsted by combined Austrian-Prussian forces and thrown back on Nogent in a snow-storm; but he turned this to good account, for the enemy now advanced separately up the Marne and the Seine and he attacked them in detail. Having trounced a Russian corps of Blücher's army at Montmirail, south-west of Eperney on the Marne (when a M. Moët produced magnums of champagne for the army), Napoleon then heavily defeated Blücher, who lost

171

ten thousand casualties at Vauchamps. He then turned on Schwarzenberg who had got as far as Montreuil south of Paris on the Seine, and defeated the Austrians, who fell back and suggested an armistice.

But the campaign in March went awry; by mid-February Wellington, by-passing Bayonne, had crossed the Adour and attacked Orthez and was forcing Soult back north-east on to Toulouse. Based on Troyes on the Seine, Napoleon now struck north to finish off the Prussians before the Austrians rallied; but he was left in the lurch because the French commander at Soissons on the Aisne surrendered. So at Craonne and Laon, north-east of Paris, Napoleon had no base at Soissons behind him, and though he evicted the Russians from Rheims, where the French kings had been crowned for centuries, when he turned south again to deal with the Austrians, he had diminished striking power. At Arcis-sur-Aube, on the way to Troyes, he had fought with suicidal courage himself, but, if his intention was to finish everything and leave the succession to his heir, it failed.

With a greatly diminished army, Napoleon now made east to St Dizier, to threaten the enemies' communications with Germany from Lorraine, but the Allies left him to it and closed in on Paris, and after the brief combat in Montmartre, on the night of 30 March, the city surrendered. Napoleon hurried back to Fontainebleau to be told, on the morning of the 31st, of the accomplished fact. He at once ordered the Regent, the King of Rome and the government to leave Paris, but only the Court obeyed him and left for Blois on the Loire; a government was left in being to treat, if it could, independently with the Allies. Marie Louise had been frightened for the child's safety, and incapable of the kind of decisions Napoleon desired: the field was left wide open for Talleyrand, who, as Vice-Grand Elector, on 1 April 1814 set up a kind of government and induced the Senate to decree Napoleon's deposition.

The brittleness of the internal Napoleonic regime now became apparent. It had always been based on the army, and like a late Roman Emperor, Napoleon had been in the last resort dependent on his officers. They naturally refused to attack Paris, for these princes and dukes of the cosmopolitan empire had too much to lose, and on 4 April at Fontainebleau, they made their own *coup* in classical Praetorian style. They crowded in upon him led by Lefebvre, his collaborator in the coup of *Brumaire*; Ney, who had done prodigies in covering the retreat from Moscow, and Berthier,

OPPOSITE The departure of Napoleon for the island of Elba on 20 April 1814: an engraving by L. Beyer after F. P. Reinhold's original watercolour.

172

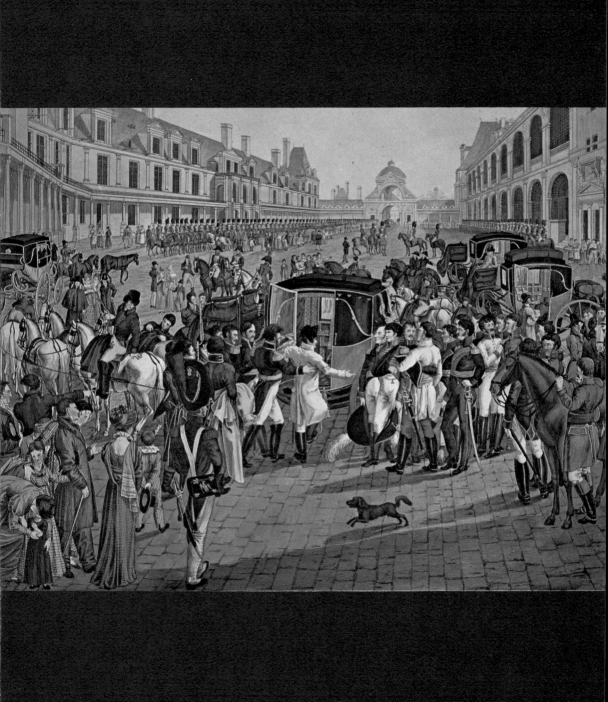

Marshal Ney, painted by Gérard. He was a brave commander but wavered in his allegiance to Napoleon.

his Chief of Staff since the first Italian campaign, and they declared that 'The army' would now 'obey only its generals'. Napoleon preserved an icy calm; but inwardly he was undecided. First he abdicated but then he tried false geniality – 'Bah, gentlemen, let's drop this and march on Paris!' He spoke of retiring to the Loire for a last resistance, then issued his farewell proclamation to the armies.

All was not yet quite lost. Talleyrand now held the cards, but he had not yet played the decisive one. Caulaincourt was well in with the Tsar, who was staying in Talleyrand's house, but no one knew how the autocrat's mind might turn: he might even try to replace Napoleon by Bernadotte. Wellington, now about to attack Toulouse, which he was to enter after heavy fighting on 12 April, did not yet assume that the Bourbons would come back, and there still seemed a chance for a Regency for Napoleon's son. Caulaincourt, backed by Marshals Ney and MacDonald, told the Tsar that the restoration of the Bourbons would mean civil war; neither the majority of the French people nor the army would accept them. But Talleyrand, now determined to work his passage home with the royalists, to whom he was heavily committed, thought that he would be safer, and France safer, under the old monarchy.

On 6 April, after a new Constitution had been drafted to reconcile the monarchy with the more moderate aspects of the Revolution, but which was not in fact imposed on the King but granted as an 'act of Grace' after the Restoration, the 'French people freely call[ed] to the throne of France Louis-Stanislas-Xavier of France, brother of the last king – and after him the other members of the House of Bourbon in the old order'. On 24 April Louis xviii, gout-ridden and obese, who had forgotten nothing and learned very little, but who was not without some pragmatic shrewdness, arrived at Calais.

Napoleon, on 12 April 1814, the day after the Treaty of Fontainebleau had guaranteed him the government of Elba, and on which Wellington had entered Toulouse, had attempted suicide. Whether he did so out of nihilist despair or even felt a twinge of guilt, it is idle to speculate. Like Hitler, he took this ghastly decision, though, unlike Hitler, he did not face certain death, but an honourable retirement already agreed. Yet he had a brilliant mind, immense gusto for life and was only forty-four. He was, of course, cut off from his wife and son, deserted now

174

Sir Thomas Lawrence's portrait of the Prussian general, Prince Gebhard Blücher. At the time of Napoleon's projected trip to the USA, Blücher swore blind that he would shoot him if he captured him.

even by Roustam and his valet; only Caulaincourt remained, and Napoleon told him that his life had become intolerable.

That night he took the poison he had carried with him on the Moscow campaign; a mixture of opium, hellebore and belladonna, nicely calculated, on his own orders, to kill two men – and probably a horse. But either because it was too strong for his system to assimilate, or because after its peregrinations in Russia,

175

central Europe and France the phial had lost its virtue, Napoleon, after hideous suffering, vomited it up. So Waterloo had to be fought and exile in St Helena suffered.

In those politically more civilized days one did not hunt down, shoot or judicially hang the leaders of defeated states, follow the ancient customs of Asian conquerors and trample them with elephants or, as in Roman times, throw them to the beasts. After all, Napoleon was the son-in-law of the most august of dynasties, and while most of the peoples concerned would gladly have lynched him, the monarchs and oligarchs were mainly determined to suppress the Revolution and restore the 'public law of Europe' buttressed by the Balance of Power.

It would not look well, indeed it might question all authority, to shoot or hang an Emperor, however parvenu. So the victors had looked about for a convenient principality with which to console the fallen dynast, and they had lighted on Elba. It was, after all, near Corsica, the birthplace of the adventurer, with a Mediterranean climate; it was in reach of Italy, and it was not, as a Greek island would have been, a spring board for adventures in the east. Nor was it, like St Helena, already advocated by the British, cut off from civilization. What world celebrity would not be grateful to settle down and write his memoirs in peace?

In fact, the Allies could hardly have chosen a worse place. Napoleon was not that sort of man, and he was already playing a political hand. He staged a lachrymose farewell to his Old Guard. On 20 April, on a cold day, he left the Cour des Adieux – the Courtyard of Farewell – in a haze of sentiment. The Allied Commissioners all wept; save, of course, the Russians. He was allowed to take a thousand of the Old Guard, and some more of them followed him later by way of Italy: Napoleon is said to have remarked *sotto voce* that with the violets he would return. And though, on his passage through royalist Provence, he was savagely attacked by the populace, lost his nerve, as in the Orangerie at St Cloud, refused food for fear of poison and even changed into an Austrian uniform, he escaped that sort of retribution. But it must have been with relief that at Fréjus he boarded the English frigate *Undaunted*, and set about charming Captain Ussher with an 'unfailing cordiality and condescension'. The English sailors kindly made up some flags for him for his new sovereignty. Napoleon was officially deemed to be descended from the dukes of Tuscany, and he adopted an old Florentine standard, surcharged with three imperial bees.

8 The Hundred Days 1815

Long life and prosperity on the Island of Elba and better luck next time.

THE BOATSWAIN OF *HMS Undaunted* ON BEHALF OF THE SHIP'S CREW

THE ISOLA D'ELBA, little more than eighteen miles long and twelve miles wide, consists mainly of wooded and serrated hills, rising in the west to nearly 3,500 feet round Monte Cappone. Its farms and olive groves spread out in the more level country behind Portoferraio on the northern coast, whose fine harbour is guarded by the fort and sea-walls built in the mid-sixteenth century by Cosimo dei Medici, Duke of Florence. Today the island contains fewer than thirty thousand people, and in Napoleon's times it supported about eleven thousand. The Etruscans and Romans had mined the iron ore, but the island's realizable assets were its farms and fisheries.

Napoleon's own residence, the pink and cream Palazzino degli Molini, is small but attractive, on its eminence behind the town, with a terrace of orange-trees and oleanders, the cliff falling away steeply on the north side to the Mediterranean. Napoleon also had a pleasant summer residence inland, and the climate was rather better than that of neighbouring Corsica.

A less daemonic character might have been content with such retirement and settled down as a celebrity and sage, writing his memoirs, receiving distinguished visitors; in general, cultivating his garden. But he still retained the title of Emperor with its memories of a vast European domination, and so tame an anti-climax seemed cowardice. What was more, Marie-Louise had

been assigned, not the neighbouring duchy of Tuscany, but that of Parma and Piacenza, and side-tracked by the Austrian Court who had thoughtfully provided her with an escort, the Count von Neipperg, who quickly became her lover. Moreover, in May 1814 Josephine, who might have visited Napoleon, had died of pneumonia, aged fifty-one; she had won the high favour and protection of the Tsar, been allowed to stay at Malmaison, and left a fortune of over nine million francs, of which six million went to her children after her debts had been paid.

Madame Mère and the Princess Borghese, who had sold her superb house in Paris (which has been the British Embassy ever since) to the Duke of Wellington when he had been appointed ambassador, arrived on Elba in July; and, as already recorded, Marie Walewska, with her four-year-old boy Alexander, had early paid a brief and secret visit. Napoleon threw himself at once into improving the economy and the communications of the island, kept all the state and protocol that he could and, only seven miles from Italy, watched political developments in France and central Europe like a hawk.

They seemed promising: the Alliance, like that between East and West in the Second World War, was already breaking down over the settlement of Germany and Poland; the English and the Austrians, no more than the French, liked having Cossacks in Paris or the powerful presence of an unpredictable Russian Tsar; Talleyrand was edging France towards being accepted as a collaborator with England, while Prussia was only reluctantly under Russian political domination. In January 1815, a secret treaty had been signed by Great Britain, Austria and France, pledging them all not to make a separate peace. Against this background, which made the Congress of Vienna more celebrated for its social brilliance than for its political harmony or decisions, the Bourbons had been making themselves extremely unpopular in France, and the disbanded veterans of Napoleon's army looked back on their exploits as the English after the Restoration had 'reflected upon Oliver' and the great things he had done. Many looked to their marshals, some of whom had hopes of a *coup d'état*.

According to Chateaubriand, Louis XVIII, known to the English as 'Bungy' (India rubber) Louis, had been received by the Imperial Guard with grimaces and grinding of teeth, and they had 'presented arms with a movement of fury'. He had insisted on superseding the tricolour by the white Bourbon cockade; and what was much worse, some of the returned émigrés were threatening to upset

181

George Cruikshank's cartoon of Louis XVIII, the representative of the restored Bourbon monarchy.

the land settlement by reclaiming unsold 'national' lands. Some of the great aristocrats had learned and forgotten as little as had the Bourbons, and the settlement of the Revolution which Napoleon had underwritten seemed in danger.

If the outlook on the continent looked more favourable, the situation on Elba had deteriorated: the promised subsidy of two million francs had not been paid, and Napoleon's own four millions which he had brought from Paris were running out; the income from Elba was negligible. There were rumours that in Vienna the statesmen were considering packing Napoleon off to the Azores, to the fever-haunted West Indies, or even St Helena, an island in the South Atlantic then known vaguely as a supply station for East Indiamen bound for Bombay, Calcutta or the Far East. Napoleon also feared assassination, and Madame Mère, always game for a fight, told him that he was 'not destined to die on this island'. Maybe his extremer enemies were encouraging their quarry to bolt.

And bolt he did. On 26 February 1815, the brig *Inconstant*, the sole vessel of Napoleon's navy, with auxiliary feluccas, stole out of Portoferraio in the dark and, favoured by a southerly wind, made Golfe Juan on 1 March, just as the violets were well out on the Riviera coast.

He was not well received by the *Maire*; 'We were just beginning to find content and tranquillity', he grumbled, 'and you are going to upset it all.' But Napoleon's spectacular success was a masterpiece of political warfare. He had with him only about a thousand men, but his main strength was in the support of the peasants and villagers, who detested the Bourbon regime, and from the first he tried to appear to them as a radical embodiment of the original Revolution, not as an established dynast. His gestures, even the apparently dangerous ones, were calculated beforehand; and when, choosing the route up by Grasse behind Cannes through the Basses Alps through Digne, Sisteron and the Grenoble gap to avoid royalist Provence, he was confronted near Laffrey by a regiment blocking the approach to Vizelle and the town, Napoleon walked forward alone in the famous grey overcoat and shouted, 'If you want to, kill your Emperor!' The risky gesture was probably a put-up job, since the troops had been already infiltrated by Napoleon's agents.

From Grenoble, he descended on the great city of Lyons, where the populace sang the *Marseillaise* and many veterans came in to his colours as he issued proclamations for radical constitutional change. Now with fourteen thousand men, he made at once for Paris. On 19 March Louis XVIII fled from the capital to Ghent, saying that the Revolution had come again, and on 20 March 1815, Napoleon was carried shoulder-high into the entrance of the Tuileries, with the radicals of Paris and the army roaring their applause.

In fact, the situation was very precarious: Napoleon had at once reappointed the ruthless but secretly hostile Fouché as Chief of Police, and Carnot, the ablest administrator, as Minister of the Interior; even the impetuous Ney, who had sworn to bring the Emperor back in a 'cage', had come over to him at Auxerre-sur-Yonne: but the middle classes, the solid body of interest and opinion who had backed him under the Consulate, were now weary of military adventure and wary of Napoleon's new radical stance. A bogus ceremony on 1 June on the Champ de Mai, when Napoleon and his three brothers appeared in the full costumes of the Empire, roused little enthusiasm. Most of the French had had more than enough.

Apprised on 7 March of what Castlereagh called 'the unfortunate evasion of that person from Elba', the politicians and diplomats at Vienna had at first treated it as a joke: they soon changed their tune and on 13 March proclaimed Napoleon an outlaw – in medieval parlance a man with a wolf's head. And Talleyrand had arranged that the proclamation had been against Napoleon personally, not against France.

On 25 March the Great Powers, now reunited, formally re-asserted their Alliance, and Wellington was made Commander-in-Chief of the British, the Belgian and the Dutch forces in Flanders.

The campaign of Waterloo is generally thought foredoomed, for even had Napoleon won it, as he very nearly did, he would have then had to fight Austrian and Russian invasions and a renewal of the English blockade and war at sea. Yet, had he won and defeated further invasion with the French fighting on their own soil and solid behind him, he might have had just enough bargaining power to have remained ruler of France; for in those days the objective was not to ruin and partition a vanquished country but to restore the European balance. But the question of Belgium would surely have remained; and it was suitable that a war which, for England, had always turned on that climatically and socially mediocre country, so long the cockpit of Europe, should have ended there.

Napoleon's worst weakness was internal. Even when 'out-lawed', he might have defied the world if the French still had the élan of the Revolution; but decades of war and conscription had left their mark, and contrary to popular belief, the core of France, as Seignobos has observed, is pacific. The peasants and bourgeoisie were concerned with *sécurité*, whatever the martial and naval traditions of glory in a state which had long had the largest population in the West. Napoleon's attempt to appear the embodi-ment of the revived Revolution had cut both ways. Few thought the regime would last: only the army and some of the generals were behind Napoleon; though, had he won the battle of Waterloo, many would doubtless have rallied to the side of the victor.

The Allies were now thoroughly alarmed. The English had, of course, promptly demobilized or dispersed the fine army that Wellington had trained and commanded in Spain, and the Duke himself had been careful, as ambassador in Paris, to appear among the glittering cavalcade of royalty in civilian coat and top hat.

184

Some of the best troops had been sent to America, where the pointless war of 1812-14 dragged on; and many had perished, along with their commander, Sir Edward Pakenham, outside New Orleans, when the war was in fact over.

The forces immediately available in Belgium were thus inadequate and heterogeneous, and the army which Wellington commanded at Waterloo contained many more Belgians, Dutch and Hanoverians than British. But in the overall strategic picture, the Allied armies vastly outnumbered the French: Napoleon had no allies, for Murat's final gamble when he reverted to Napoleon's side and led a Neapolitan army against the Austrians had ended early in May at Tolentino.

In the whole Campaign which ended at Waterloo, Napoleon had no more than 122,000 men, set against 120,000 Prussians, 70,000 from Hanover and the Low Countries, and 30,000 British. Plainly the only political and strategic chance was to strike at once. Intending, in his accustomed way, to crush first one enemy then the other, he left Paris on 12 June, after dining with some of his family the night before and remarking with disarming

The Congress of Vienna after a painting by Isabey. Castlereagh is to be seen in the centre, partly obscured by a chair, and looking towards Wellington (left foreground).

185

The Battle of Waterloo

Waterloo, the final act in the drama of Napoleon's quest for European domination, was fought under the shadow of ill health and limited support from the army and its generals. Napoleon's troops proved to be no match for the combined forces of the Allies in strength, numbers or initiative. Once again he deserted them after defeat.

RIGHT Arthur Wellesley, 1st Duke of Wellington: Henry Guttman's portrait of the brilliant English commander.

BELOW *The Fight for the Standard. Battle of Waterloo* by Ansdell: Sergeant Eward of the Scots Greys seizes the 'Eagle' from the French 45th regiment.

LEFT The observatory from which Napoleon viewed the battle.

BELOW Napoleon charges through the mêlée.

candour, 'If only we don't live to regret Elba!' The army was hastily mobilized, ill found and without nearly all of the marshals on whom Napoleon had relied; Berthier, his Chief of Staff, was dead, having left France and thrown himself from a window in Baden twelve days before. Soult, who had shown his lethargy and limitations in Spain, was a poor substitute, while Murat had now lost all credibility and Napoleon had refused to see him. Ney, always a better fighter than strategist, had not now much credibility either, Grouchy was a cavalry commander, without experience of higher responsibility and a political appointment, and d'Erlon lacked initiative.

The classic Napoleonic battle demanded lucid grasp of strategy, intelligent collaboration in tactics and subordinates able to improvise in a crisis. At Waterloo they showed none of these qualities. And although his own strategy was correct and brilliantly conceived, the Emperor, no longer fully himself, showed an unwonted hesitation and even misplaced caution.

The essential point which Napoleon had grasped was that the Prussians were based on Namur on the Meuse and the British and their allies on Antwerp and Ostend, and that between them ran the main road from France through Charleroi to Brussels.

Napoleon soon won the first advantage: having successfully sealed off the frontiers – in those days a remarkable feat – he had swiftly concentrated his armies on the Sambre around Beaumont without either Blücher's or Wellington's knowledge. He was thus poised to strike north, as he intended, at the gap between their armies, with the option of swinging west, enveloping Wellington's army and cutting them off from Ostend and perhaps Antwerp, on the face of it the more attractive possibility, since many of the Belgian *haute-bourgeoisie* were pro-French. So he feinted to do so, but struck at the Prussians to knock them out first.

Very early and rapidly on 15 June, Napoleon advanced into Belgium and drove the Prussians out of Charleroi, but Wellington considered that the real attack might still come on Mons to the west, aiming at his own west flank. And when a delayed message informed him that the Prussians were taking the main thrust north-east, at Ligny, while the French were also advancing rapidly on the Brussels road to attack his centre through Frasnes and Les Quatre Bras, he remarked, 'Napoleon has humbugged me, by God! He has gained twenty-four hours march on me.' Early on 16 June the French were at Frasnes and, later that morning, Wellington arrived at Les Quatre Bras, where the road from

Namur crosses that from Charleroi to Brussels. He was now six miles from Blücher at Ligny on the Ligne and he at once rode out to concert their strategy, returning with a promise of mutual support as circumstances would demand.

Early in the afternoon, Napoleon attacked the Prussians with devastating force, inflicting sixteen thousand casualties in an attempt to disrupt their centre, envelop them on the left and drive them east — away from Wellington. But Ney, over-impetuous, had tried to overrun Wellington's army at Les Quatre Bras, not just to pin it down. He had not the force to break them and they were hourly being reinforced, so that he was too fully engaged to help destroy the Prussians. Further, when the Count d'Erlon, though in reserve to Ney with twenty thousand men, had begun under orders from one of Napoleon's staff to march on the Prussian flank — a correct move — Ney belatedly countermanded it, so that d'Erlon, who might have finished off the Prussians, marched and counter-marched to no effect. Neither Wellington nor Blücher was overwhelmed, though the Prussians had been badly mauled and Blücher himself, aged seventy-six, charging at the head of his cavalry, was unhorsed and ridden over, leaving the less reliable Gneisenau in brief command. But early on the 17th at Les Quatre Bras, Wellington made a crucial decision: 'Old Blücher', he said, 'has had a damned good licking and has gone back to Wavre, eighteen miles. As he has gone back, we must too.' For Blücher had not fallen back on Namur, the line of retreat to Germany; he meant still to defend Brussels. So Wellington conformed and ordered a retreat to the position he had already surveyed at Waterloo.

This prompt decision saved the campaign, and Napoleon soon knew it; his strategy of defeating first the Prussians then Wellington was now jeopardized. With a curious lethargy, the Emperor had neither fully followed up the Prussian retreat nor at once thrown his main force behind Ney; and the latter, too, had wasted the crucial morning of 17 June. When, at 2 p.m., Napoleon at last arrived at Les Quatre Bras, he found that Wellington's army had evaded him. The Prussians had not been routed nor the British and the Allies overwhelmed. With succinct lucidity, Napoleon already observed of Ney, 'On a perdu la France' — 'France is lost.'

But if his strategy had failed, Napoleon had a good tactical chance left: a total attack on Wellington's position while the Prussians were still crippled and perhaps even retreating east on Namur. Having already ordered Grouchy, with thirty-three

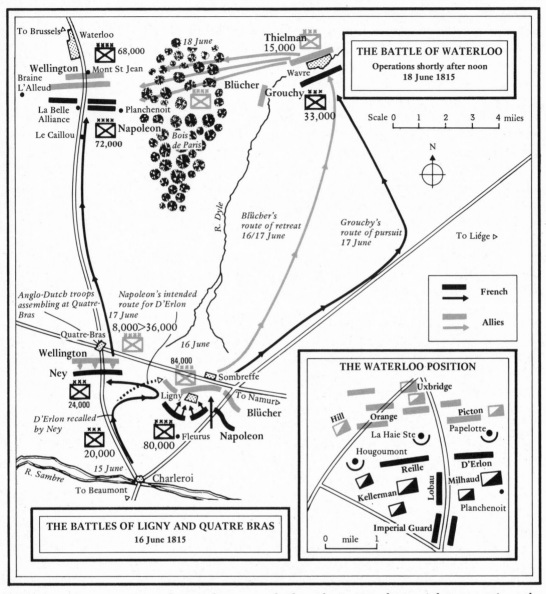

To Brussels ◁
Waterloo
68,000
Wellington
Braine
L'Alleud
Mont St Jean
La Belle
Alliance
Le Caillou
Planchenoit
Napoleon
72,000
Bois
de Paris

18 June
Thielman
15,000
Blücher
Wavre
Grouchy
33,000

THE BATTLE OF WATERLOO
Operations shortly after noon
18 June 1815

Scale 0   1   2   3   4 miles

N

R. Dyle

Blücher's
route of retreat
16/17 June

Grouchy's
route of pursuit
17 June

To Liége ▷

Anglo-Dutch troops
assembling at Quatre-
Bras
17 June
8,000 > 36,000

Napoleon's intended
route for D'Erlon

French

Allies

Quatre-Bras
Wellington
Ney
24,000

D'Erlon recalled
by Ney

20,000

R. Sambre
15 June

To Beaumont ▷

16 June
84,000

80,000

Ligny
Fleurus

Sombreffe
To Namur ▷
Blücher

Napoleon

Charleroi

THE BATTLE OF WATERLOO POSITION

Uxbridge
Hill
Orange
La Haie Ste
Hougoumont
Picton
Papelotte
Reille
Lobau
D'Erlon
Milhaud
Kellerman
Planchenoit
Imperial Guard

0   mile   1

THE BATTLES OF LIGNY AND QUATRE BRAS
16 June 1815

thousand men, to shadow them, Napoleon might yet retrieve the
campaign by smashing Wellington. And this in the final bombardment and assault he very nearly did.

As often in Belgium, it was a sultry summer, and on 17 June
the weather had broken in a great thunderstorm which had
hindered the French from catching Wellington; by the evening
he was at Mont St Jean, rising ground in the undulating country
south of Waterloo. Here, relying on Prussian help by the early

190

afternoon, Wellington prepared a defensive battle. Warned of his qualities, Napoleon remarked, 'I tell you that Wellington is a bad general, that the English are bad troops, it will be a picnic.' But Grouchy, who had already reported that Prussian forces were at Wavre, was later bewildered by ambiguous orders, so that he neither at once put in a decisive attack on Wavre which might have spoiled the Prussian advance, nor rejoined Napoleon. Had Grouchy's men been available against Wellington the battle might have had a different outcome.

The gently rolling and fertile country at Mont St Jean and Waterloo, now distinguished by some hideous memorials (but, strangely enough, none to Wellington), was then under heavy summer crops of wheat, rye and clover, and the woods were in full leaf, giving good cover. But the pouring rain had made the country sodden and added to the miseries of both armies during the night. Wellington had chosen a favourite position, with his infantry concealed on the other side of the slope – an expedient that the continentals, as had the Prussians at Ligny, considered 'not done'. British contingents had also been placed among the Hanoverian and Low Country regiments to stiffen them – not without cause, for even before the battle, a Dutch battalion from Nassau had made off. But the numbers were fairly even; Napoleon's seventy-four thousand against Wellington's sixty-seven thousand.

The Emperor began the day in apparently optimistic mood, relieved that Wellington was still there – 'Aha', he said, 'now we have them – these English!' With exalted confidence he still calculated on a ninety per cent chance in his favour. 'This affair', he said, 'is nothing more than eating breakfast.'

It was a misty Sunday morning and Napoleon, with unusual misjudgment, wasted most of the morning to let the ground dry. But as though determined to have done with the campaign one way or the other and ever reckless of life, he had decided on a bull-headed attack, and Soult had ordered Grouchy to 'march on Wavre so as to draw near to us' – a contradiction by the map. This extremely bad staff work proved disastrous, for Grouchy, a prudent subordinate, continued to march on Wavre. Meanwhile, the French made an intimidating, dramatic and splendid show in a cosmopolitan variety of uniforms against the skirl and thunder of their bands, as for the last time they marched past the Emperor.

The preliminary bombardment was intense, for the French out-gunned Wellington; and when at 1.30 p.m. Ney opened the frontal attack, the first with infantry, the second with cavalry, the outcome of the battle hung in the balance. But these tactics proved disastrous: the infantry columns withered under the British and Allied fire and provoked violent cavalry counter-attacks; the cavalry, unsupported by the horse artillery which could have blasted the squares, swirled around Wellington's infantry but predictably did not break them. And by 3 p.m. Napoleon, at his command post at La Belle Alliance farm, had received Grouchy's report that the Prussians, whose advance parties Wellington had already seen, would soon be attacking along the whole eastern flank. Napoleon now had virtually two battles on his hands; and after the failure of the French cavalry, Wellington remarked 'The battle is mine, if the Prussians arrive soon, and there will be an end to the war.'

He was right. Napoleon, to fend off the Prussians, had to divert sixteen thousand men of his reserve; and when at last, at 6.30 p.m., Ney captured La Haye Sainte, the farm buildings that had been Wellington's command post and which had held up the French attack on the Allied centre, and demanded that the Guard press home a decisive break-through, Napoleon refused the risk. An hour later, he took the risk, and Wellington's tactics were too much for him. For as the bear-skinned, blue-coated professionals advanced up the slope to the menacing tattoo of their drums and topped the crest, the British First Footguards, who had lain concealed, rose and confronted them at forty yards and poured in volleys so devastating that even the Guards recoiled. Whereat the British 52nd, on their flank, rose out of the standing corn and raked them as well. And all this time, the Prussians had been closing in, so that by 7.30 they had crashed into Napoleon's right. Wellington, now back at La Haye Sainte and conspicuous in the light of the declining sun, waved his hat three times towards the French: 'Damn it,' he remarked, 'in for a penny in for a pound.' The British and Allied armies surged down the slope, as the Prussians pressed home their massive attack.

The French were now broken. Morale had gone. 'La Garde recule' had given way to 'nous sommes trahis'. Only the final uncommitted battalions of the Old Guard remained to escort the Emperor as he left the field. It was now 9 p.m. when, south of La Belle Alliance, Blücher and Wellington greeted one another, while Napoleon fled from his army in his elaborate dark blue bullet-proof travelling carriage. It was singularly well-equipped, with 'close on a hundred pieces from a splendidly appointed travelling case, nearly all in solid gold, two leather bottles, one of rum and

another of fine old Malaga, a million francs' worth of diamonds and a cake of Windsor soap'. Pursued by Prussian cavalry, the Emperor soon took swifter flight on horseback, and, guarded by lancers, rode all night till he came to Charleroi in the dawn. The carnage of the battle, fought in such a small area, had been frightful; between forty and fifty thousand casualties, twenty-five thousand of them French: 'the most desperate business', wrote Wellington, 'I ever was in: I never took so much trouble about any battle, and never was so near being beat.' He would also declare, 'I have fought the French as often as anybody, and I will say this for them, that I never saw them behave ill except at the end of the Battle of Waterloo.' Most famously, he said, 'It was a damn'd near run thing.'

Napoleon, as in Egypt and in Russia, had left his army for very good political reasons. France had never been solid behind him, and he well knew the welter of intrigue that the news of the catastrophe would set off in Paris. Early on the morning of 21 June

An engraving after the well-known painting of *Wellington and Blücher meeting after the Battle of Waterloo* by Daniel Maclise. As they shook hands, Napoleon was making a hasty getaway. Maclise started work on his canvas in 1858.

193

– Midsummer's Day – he was back in the luxurious Elysée Palace, where he got straight into a hot bath and stayed long there. The Legislature was already in session and up to no good, and he was pressed to dissolve it by force. But Fouché, the regicide Chief of Police, determined, like Talleyrand, to work his passage home, had initiated a decree that to dissolve the Legislature would be treason. Lafayette had reappeared and led the demand for abdication. Lucien urged his brother to resist. Carnot, too, urged him to lead the other armies which could be regrouped on the Loire and rally the country by the slogan *'La Patrie en danger!'* But next day Napoleon dictated his abdication:

Frenchmen, when I began the war to maintain our national independence, I counted on the union of every effort and will, on the help of every national authority, I had good reason to hope for success. . . . Circumstances seem to have changed. I offer myself as a sacrifice to the hatred of the enemies of France. . . . My political life is over, and I proclaim my son Emperor of the French with the title of Napoleon II. May you all unite for the salvation of the nation and for the independence of France.

Fouché at once delivered the declaration to Lafayette: on the Bourse, where the French *Rentes* had already risen by two francs, they now rose by 4.50 francs. Carnot still wanted to install Napoleon II, but in spite of Bonapartist demonstrations round the Elysée, Napoleon remained irresolute, played out.

Then, on the evening of 23 June, he decided to make for the United States. He gave orders that the fast frigates *Saale* and *Meduse* were to be prepared at Rochefort on the Charente, on the Atlantic coast behind the Ile d'Oleron; and on 25 June he left the Elysée for Malmaison, eight miles outside Paris, now the property of Hortense, ex-Queen of Holland, and where, in the miniature elegance created by Josephine, he longed to rest and recuperate. He saw Marie Walewska and her son, and other intimates, for the last time. Then he turned to business, and made dispositions which secured six million francs, not, in the event, for himself, but for his heirs: the furnishings of two considerable households were got together with a selection made from his personal library, and Napoleon's doctor provided him with a new poison, guaranteed this time to work, which he would keep till he got to St Helena.

By 28 June the infuriated old Blücher, who had fits of madness when he thought he was pregnant with an elephant, and who had sworn to have Napoleon shot and would probably have carried

Vendramini's engraving of the drawing of Joseph Fouché, Duke of Otranto by P. E. Stroehling. One of Napoleon's worst mistakes was to include this intriguer in the government he formed before Waterloo.

out his threat, was advancing on Paris. Next day, with a final surge of pugnacity, Napoleon appeared dressed as a Colonel of the Riflemen of the Guard, and offered his services to the provisional government as a general to defend France on the Loire. They turned him down. For now even Fouché was wanting to be rid of him, and permits for the frigates to sail had been accorded. So Napoleon took a last long look at Josephine's room, then stoically parted from his mother and from his step-daughter Hortense. He would never again see either of them.

The convoy of ten carriages now set off, Napoleon himself travelling separately to avoid recognition, in civilian clothes and round hat in a plain barouche. He took the road to the south-west, by Rambouillet, where he stayed a night; to Chartres where the great fields were white for harvest; and on to Vendôme and Tours; then, south of the Loire, in the full heat of summer, on to Poitiers and Niort, where, since his government had drained the marshes, he was wildly acclaimed. On 3 July he arrived at Rochefort.

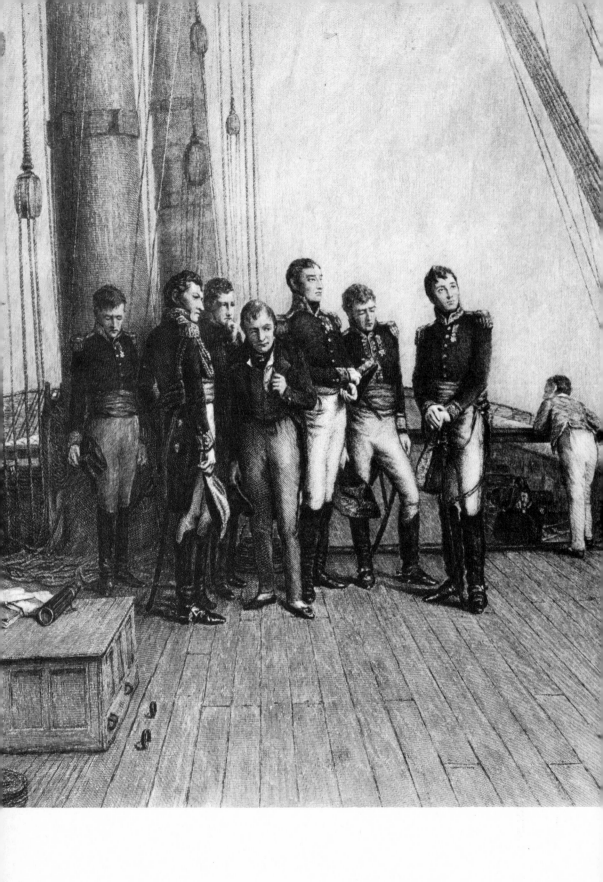

A familiar representation of
Napoleon aboard the
Bellerophon, watched by
English officers who
accorded him royal treatment:
W. Q. Orchardson's painting,
engraved by J. C. Armytage.

A few hours after he had left, Prussian troops had appeared at Malmaison. Rochefort, too, was Bonapartist, but Fouché was negotiating at Neuilly with Wellington and Talleyrand so that he would be included as Minister of Police, as would Talleyrand as President of the Council and Minister for Foreign Affairs in the government of Louis XVIII. No one had more experience in this vital aspect of administration; moreover, as Talleyrand remarked after Fouché had drawn up the list of those prescribed, 'One must do him the justice to recognize that he has omitted none of his friends.'

Napoleon dared not linger in Rochefort; and on the afternoon of 8 July, at the fishing village of Fouras opposite the sandy pine-clad Ile d'Oleron, the Emperor left the mainland of France for ever to board the frigate *Saale*, carried on the back of a stalwart fisherman because the Atlantic tide in the estuary was out and the boats could not come inshore. He was received with proper formality and well accommodated, and on that very day Louis XVIII returned to Paris.

Here Napoleon remained for five days. It was alleged that the British were off the straits between the Ile d'Oleron and the Ile de Ré; in fact, they were so far spread out between Brest and the Gironde estuary that the chances of escape to America were still good. Even when HMS *Bellerophon*, seventy-four guns, which had fought at Abuqīr Bay and Trafalgar, closed in, the two French frigates nearly made a run for it, the *Meduse* to engage while the *Saale* got away. But the covertly royalist captain of the *Saale* baulked at the last minute; and on 13 July Napoleon, distrusting him, took refuge on the Ile d'Aix, two miles off Fouras. Here he met ex-King Joseph, who had chartered an American brig at Royan at the mouth of the Gironde estuary. This scheme was superseded by the offer of the explorer Baudin, who had arranged, in collaboration with the American consul at Bordeaux, a passage for Napoleon on an American clipper, the *Pike*. It lay off Le Verdon at the tip of the Medoc peninsula, and was so fast that it could have evaded all pursuit. Joseph even offered to impersonate Napoleon while he got away; but Napoleon refused the subterfuge, which he thought beneath him: if he went, he would go only with a proper entourage. And when the Dutch schooner *Magdelaine* was discovered, bound for Boston, he again insisted that his suite follow; this time in converted coasting luggers, which would transfer them to some merchant ship once off the coast.

On the night of 13-14 July, this last plan went ahead. Then, finally, Napoleon changed his mind: very early on the 14th he sent envoys to *Bellerophon* to ask for passage to the United States, a request he must surely have known to be impracticable; or, if it were refused, to ask passage for himself and his entourage to England. Having conquered much of the Old World, it seems that Napoleon, when it came to it, could not face the New. He thought he might be assassinated there by royalist agents, and he deluded himself with the prospect of a comfortable retirement in the one part of Europe which he hoped that he had not made too hot to hold him.

The English lost no time: by 10 a.m. Captain Maitland, having refused the first proposition, acceded to the second, and Napoleon went on board. With singular miscalculation of political realities in England, Napoleon had already written out his message, as of one head of state to another, to the Prince Regent:

Your Royal Highness. Exposed as I am to the factions that divide my country, and to the enmity of the Greater Powers of Europe, I have ended my political career, and come, like Themistocles, to sit by the hearth of the British people. I put myself under the protection of their laws, which I ask from your Royal Highness as the most powerful, the most constant, and the most generous of my enemies. Napoleon. *The Isle of Aix. 13th July, 1815.*

The message was written in an idiom calculated to make Frenchmen weep, and, indeed, to move the emotional Prince Regent, though officially he was not aware of Napoleon's existence, only of a General Bonaparte: but seldom has the contrast between the French and English styles been more apparent. To the hard-bitten oligarchy that ruled Great Britain and who more than anyone else had brought Napoleon down, it seemed theatrical and politically irrelevant. How many divisions had Napoleon now?

9 The Prisoner of St Helena 1815-21

Do you suppose that when I wake at night I have not bad
moments – when I think of what I was and what I am?

NAPOLEON

WHEN IN THE EARLY DAWN OF 15 July, a longboat from *Bellerophon*, on orders from Captain Maitland, determined to forestall his Admiral who was coming in under full sail, took Napoleon and his suite off the brig *Épervier* as it laboured against a shift of wind, and brought them alongside the great striped yellow and black hull, he had escaped only by a hairbreadth and the devotion of his partisans from the clutches of a royalist *préfet* who had just arrived at Rochefort.

His decision taken, Napoleon cheered up and set himself to charm his captors. Those who expected an ogre or a gaunt predator were surprised by the short, stout, sturdy figure who came aboard in the dark green uniform coat with the red collar over white waistcoat and breeches, his olive complexion 'more like an obese Spanish or Portuguese friar than the hero of modern times'. Captain (afterwards Rear Admiral Sir Frederick) Maitland had turned out only a general's guard of honour, but he was all civility, and he spoke French. His instructions had been to prevent Bonaparte's escape, and in the preliminary negotiation he had painted the prospects in England as better than he knew them to be: it is not every day that a Scots career officer and younger son has the chance to bag a world conqueror.

So Napoleon's natural and irrepressible élan and optimism revived. He had been assigned the big after-cabin where he showed off his portable camp bed, and next morning he went aboard HMS *Superb*, Admiral Hotham's flagship, where he was entertained in royal style. As in *Bellerophon*, he laid himself out to charm; flattering the Admiral on the silence and order of the great ship of the line, contrasting, he said, with the more voluble and apparently confused methods of the French navy.

On 16 July *Bellerophon* weighed anchor and in brisk fine weather sailed for England. When they made Ushant at the extreme west of Brittany, Napoleon stayed on deck from five o'clock till midday watching through his pocket glass the last of the coast of France. In spite of the melancholy occasion, the enforced rest and the good air put him in a better shape after the hectic anxieties of the Hundred Days; and he enjoyed the amateur theatricals customary in the Royal Navy during their long months at sea, remarking how well the young midshipmen acted as girls. He discussed English country life with Maitland (he had packed a variety of sporting guns) and he had high hopes of being allowed to settle as 'Colonel Muiron' on an English estate. These hopes were encouraged by a friendly reception at Torbay and Plymouth,

where the English civilians characteristically came out in thousands for a glimpse of the fallen Emperor, and raised their hats to him and even cheered instead of greeting him with execrations. In fact, this English sentiment made the Cabinet all the more determined not to harbour Napoleon in the island where, with the foreseeably growing unpopularity of the Bourbons, he would have been a focus for Bonapartist hopes and of Whig and Radical disaffection against the Tory Government. Privately some ministers deplored that he had not been shot by Blücher or hanged in France, where the restored monarch, once well in the saddle, very soon got rid of the two main architects of his restoration by making Fouché ambassador to the United States and forcing Talleyrand into retirement.

Napoleon had created devastation on a scale hitherto unknown in Europe; but since he had become a kind of royalty by marriage and consideration was still accorded between the ruling classes, his punishment for failure was relatively humane. The alleged 'martyrdom' on St Helena, miserable as it was, compared well with the fate of Mussolini, upside down like a stuck pig, or of Hitler, his brains blown out in the *Führerbunker*, or of Hess shut up for life. Yet so brilliant was Napoleon's political flair that when he had been, relatively speaking, let off, he deliberately and successfully created a Bonapartist legend which greatly contributed to the return of his dynasty to the throne of France.

'L'Angleterre', one Bonapartist would write, now *'se mit a dévorer le grand homme en plein jour'* ('England intends to eat the great man in broad daylight'). And, indeed, St Helena was a dismal place for one who had ruled from the Neva to the Tagus. It was little more than half the size of Elba, cut off from France by about five thousand, and from Africa by about 1,150, miles of the Atlantic. It has cliffs running to two thousand feet, and a half circle of volcanic mountains up to twenty-eight hundred feet which, facing south (though not the sun), break down into deep gorges cut by streams from the heavy rainfall on the windswept heights. The tropical climate, on the other hand, which Wellington, coming from India, had thought good, was tempered by the cold current of the South Atlantic, and temperatures ranged from 68° to 90° in the summer and never below 50° in winter. Today, above the sparse and prickly vegetation on the arid coast, the more sheltered middle levels of moderate rainfall sustain oaks, pines, cedars, willows and poplars, as well as eucalyptus, bananas

and bamboo. Fruit and vegetables flourish, and cattle, sheep and pigs do well, while the fisheries are varied and considerable.

It had been discovered in 1502 by the Portuguese on the festival of St Helena, mother of Constantine, and occupied by the English East India Company in 1659, who made it a main port of call and imported slave labour from Madagascar and south-east Asia. Captain Jenkins of the 'War of Jenkins's ear' had been briefly a governor, and some of the resident or semi-resident merchants were well off. In Napoleon's time, the place was less remote than it is today (there is still no air service) and the harbour of Jamestown was often full of big ships taking in fresh water and supplies *en route* to and from India and the Far East.

Though the island was by no means the hell on earth depicted by Frenchmen miserable anywhere outside France, the banishment was obviously final. And when Admiral Lord Keith had to break the 'disagreeable news' that St Helena was to be his fate, Napoleon was shocked and indignant, though it was better than being handed over to the Bourbon government. Since the Convention signed in Paris on 2 August, on the day that he had been acclaimed at Plymouth, Napoleon was technically the prisoner of all the Allies, and it had fallen to the English government to dispose of him. His rank was now considered that of a half-pay general. In Elba he had been titular Emperor, sovereign of the island, but now he was allowed only a small household: General Bertrand, a veteran of Egypt, who had been on Elba; General Charles Montholon, his aide-de-camp during the Hundred Days, and their wives; Baron Gourgaud, the youngest, most devoted and most neurotic of the soldiers, and the civilian Emmanuel-Auguste-Dieudonné Martin-Joseph, Comte de Las Cases. As the last's names indicate, he was an aristocrat and former émigré – and the only one of them who knew English. Though Bertrand's memoirs, the most reliable, and written in cypher, were not published until 1948, they all wrote memoirs of varying value and mendaciousness, Las Cases's are the most readable and least reliable (he made his fortune from them), while Gourgaud's are the most intimate.

None of these people were anywhere near Napoleon's calibre. He was without wife, children or family, his colossal and imperious egotism set by decades of power; over the years the atmosphere became increasingly tense and claustrophobic and the main enemy would be boredom. As Gourgaud put it, '*Mardi 25. Ennui! Ennui! Mercredi 26me idem. Jeudi 27me idem. Vendredi*

28me idem. Samedi 29me idem. Dimanche 30me Grand Ennui!'
On the whole, Napoleon would bear up better than the others.

HMS *Northumberland*, with Admiral Sir George Cockburn in command, was not in good shape. She had recently arrived from India, the crew were mutinous and Napoleon's cabin, hastily fitted up, was only twelve feet by nine. When, in early August, she sailed from Portsmouth, soldiers had to compel the men to weigh anchor, and a guard was set on Napoleon's cabin lest he incite the crew. Nor did he find the respect he had been accorded on *Bellerophon*: he was not allowed another cabin as a study, and the officers did not uncover when he appeared. The long English meals and the unintelligible conversation over the port bored Napoleon, who never spent long at table, and when he left early he was thought to be giving himself airs.

During the nearly three months' voyage, during which he passed his forty-sixth birthday, Napoleon tried and failed to learn English, and a later attempt at St Helena was also too much for him: 'Since sixt wek y learn the English ... after this you shall agree that the study one tongue is a great labour who it must do with the young aged.' And when at last the volcanic island came into view he was horrified. 'It is a disgraceful island,' he exclaimed, 'it is a prison' – which it was. He would have done better, he remarked revealingly, to have 'stayed in Egypt'.

At first he occupied a pavilion in the grounds of 'The Briars', the home of the East India Company's agent William Balcombe, who had two attractive daughters of sixteen and fourteen; the younger, Betsy, who could speak French, a tomboy with whom Napoleon at first got on very well. The girls gave him a salutary change from the atmosphere of grievance and jealousy with which he became increasingly surrounded and formed one of the few compensations in his exile, until they left in 1818.

After two months he moved up to Longwood House, the summer residence of the Lieutenant Governor, on a relatively healthy but windswept plateau at seventeen hundred feet. It was a spacious if dilapidated place, enlarged for Napoleon's household, and the part now lived in by the French Consul and curator is attractive today, with a fine prospect towards the forested mountains. Napoleon's apartments were small; but he had a drawing-room, a dining-room and a little billiard-room, besides a kind of study and a small bedroom with a sofa, a writing table and fireplace, and a bathroom.

He was thus not, as sometimes supposed, condemned to very

OPPOSITE The solitary and nameless tomb of Napoleon on the island of St Helena, shaded by trees.

cramped and badly furnished quarters, and he was surrounded with pictures of his family and with his most cherished possessions, including the plundered clock of Frederick the Great. He had about fifteen hundred books and bought more from Europe – his main interest. The worst disadvantage were the rats which swarmed on the island, raced above the ceilings of the rambling house and even appeared in the dining-room itself. Once one emerged from Napoleon's hat, but apparently he minded them less than one would expect. When rabbits were introduced, the rats killed them.

Externally Napoleon kept up all the state he could, with a carriage and six horses and liveried attendants, though 'The roads of St Helena were such that the ladies of his party when they went out to dinner ... had to be conveyed in a Merovingian equipage drawn by several yoke of oxen.' He could ride only a short distance without a supervision that he found intolerable, and by 1819 his main hobby became his garden – he laid out paths and made a pool for goldfish and beds of begonias and roses. One of his objects was to enlarge the boundaries to keep observers at a distance, and he would conduct his gardening like an operation of war, wearing a huge straw hat, and expecting his household, as well as his gardeners, to participate. Soldiers from the garrison were allowed to help in the heavier tasks and Chinese coolies were co-opted. There was not much game on St Helena, but Napoleon did his best by shooting any animal that might spoil his gardens, including a bullock and some goats.

Indoors he always insisted on strict ceremonial, making the generals, Las Cases and his doctor stand for hours; no one entered his room without being summoned, and his elaborate meals were served off gold and silver plate by liveried footmen; a duty to which at first some sailors from *Northumberland* were incongruously assigned. Napoleon had almost lost the habit of writing, his handwriting was appalling and he had long been used to dictate. And this he did, sometimes for hours on end and at any time; in days before shorthand, let alone mechanical aids, he exhausted his entourage. He would also read aloud, and declaim from Corneille, his favourite playwright, and from Racine: he preferred tragedy, including Voltaire's tedious *Zaïre*, but he also enjoyed Molière and Beaumarchais, and he read translations of Greek epics and drama, of Milton and Hume, and of his favourite *Ossian*. He found consolation in *Paul et Virginie*, an idyll set in Mauritius. In sum, he did his best to fight the frustration and pointlessness of his internment, but 'one is reminded of a caged animal walking restlessly and aimlessly up and down his confined den, and watching the outside world with the fierce despair of his wild eye.'

Napoleon retained one constructive ambition and purpose – to create a Bonapartist myth; and in this he succeeded. He deliberately exaggerated the miseries of an alleged martyrdom, and he

Sir Hudson Lowe, Governor of St Helena, into whose inept hands fell the task of watching over the exile: a portrait by an unknown artist.

could have had no better ally than the governor of St Helena, Sir Hudson Lowe, who took up his post in April 1816.

Lowe, one of those unfortunate mediocrities whom the chances of history have miscast, has obtained and deserved a reputation for crass ineptitude. Yet his war record had been quite good: apart from his surrender of Capri in 1808, a place one would have thought easy to defend, he had served with credit in Egypt, at Gibraltar, in Holland, on the Baltic and in France. On paper his qualifications were exceptional: the son of an army surgeon who had become director of medical services at Gibraltar, he had early travelled in Italy and France, and became proficient in French, Italian, Spanish and Portuguese. He had originally made his career under the patronage of Sir John Moore; then on peripheral appointments which others could not or would not manage – organizing royalist Corsican 'Rangers', German deserters from the retreat from Moscow on the Baltic and Dutch rebels from the Napoleonic regime in Holland. One can see just how this sort of record would appeal to the War and Colonial Offices. He had dealt with peculiar and probably tiresome foreigners, and if they had included Corsican 'Rangers' whom Napoleon was bound to detest and fear, here was the obvious man to contend with the ex-Emperor and his difficult entourage.

The authorities had made a stupid choice: the command of the Corsican 'Rangers' alone should have vetoed the appointment. The Governor's 'manner', admits his biographer, 'was not pre-possessing even in the judgement of favourable friends', and Wellington said that he 'wanted education and judgement', was no man of the world and, in short, a 'damned fool'. He quarrelled at once with Napoleon and his suite, and with the Admiral and the Commissioners, detailed to watch Napoleon's movements but who hardly ever saw him, and he upset his subordinates. He meant well, and in 1818 emancipated all the slaves in the island, but he was terrified that his captive would escape. Nearly three thousand men and some patrolling frigates were employed for six years on their unrewarding task. Napoleon detested the fussy little man who insisted on calling him 'General Bonaparte': 'His eye', he remarked, 'is that of a hyena caught in a trap.'

The perceptive and all too articulate French made verbal mincemeat of nearly everyone in the island, save the women who attracted them. By August 1816 Napoleon had quarrelled so violently with Lowe that he refused ever to see him again. Reverting to a kind of Corsican vendetta, he thought that Lowe

210

might poison him and called him not a gaoler but a 'hangman'. In the final exchange, Napoleon scored heavily; 'I am Emperor, when England and Europe are gone, when your name and Lord Bathhurst's are forgotten, I shall still be the Emperor Napoleon.' They would remain totally estranged for five years.

As these years dragged by, with what hopes of liberation he had ever had vanishing, Napoleon's natural vitality and brilliance became dimmed. In 1817 after, in a calculated gesture, he had sold some of his plate, the allowance for the household was raised to £12,000, the equivalent of Lowe's own generous, but unpensionable salary. Living on St Helena was very expensive. Then the close restriction on exercise was lifted; but Napoleon was now physically going downhill, and spent most of his time indoors, often in his bath. The quarrels and jealousies among the entourage continued. By the autumn of 1816, Las Cases had been deported for smuggling letters, and next year Gourgaud became so temperamental that he had to go – an occasion when Napoleon remarked 'After all, if one had nothing else, one would have to find one's company in a green parrot.'

There is little but tragedy in these closing years. But they are fully, if unreliably, documented, so that many of Napoleon's reflections on life and his own extraordinary past have come through. He remained resolutely agnostic: 'Were I obliged to have a religion, I would worship the sun, the source of all life – the real God of the earth.' He did not expect survival: 'When we are dead, my dear Gourgaud, we are altogether dead'; 'When I see that a pig has a stomach like mine, and digests like me, I say to myself, if I have a soul so has he. ... In my opinion we are all matter.' He seems to have considered Islam the most socially satisfactory public creed, and he thought the best way to solve the colour problem was for a man to have two wives, one white and the other coloured, so his children would have no prejudices. He may have had a vague Deistic belief, but he certainly did not believe in a benevolent providence: there was no justice in the world – 'Look how Talleyrand has prospered – he is sure to die in his bed.'

So Napoleon had not much to fall back on as he came to his end. Gradually he became more apathetic, shut himself up and did not dress until the afternoon. He now went out very little and brooded increasingly on the past; he regretted most that he had not stayed in Egypt and carved out an empire in the East. Failing that, he regretted that he had not been killed at Borodino or at

Waterloo. Reverting to his origins, he remained a man of the
eighteenth century, an enlightened despot, with a fear of and
contempt for the *canaille* – 'I will not', he had remarked during the
Hundred Days, when urged to let loose another radical revolution
of the peasants and artisans, 'I will not be the King of the Mob.'

According to the political legend of St Helena, Napoleon died
of a disease of the liver caused by the conditions on the island
and, had he been liberated, he could have recovered. By 1819 he
was indeed suffering from what an army doctor, dismissed by
Lowe for his politically damaging diagnosis, had recognized as
the prevalent *hepatitis*; but he would in fact die of cancer.
Madame Mère, now more than ever *dévote*, sent out an elderly
Corsican priest and a young Corsican doctor's assistant named
Antommachi, ignorant, conceited and inexperienced; and by
1821 the duodenal-pyloric cancer that was killing Napoleon had
developed and gave him frightful pain. When he vomited, the
Corsican gave him a tartaric emetic which caused such agony
that his patient refused his further remedies. Whereat Bertrand
called in a Scots army surgeon, who helpfully diagnosed 'hypo-
chondria'.

By 12-15 April, Napoleon, with a supreme effort, dictated an
elaborate Will, dealing with his fortune of more than seven and
a half million francs, most of it still in Paris, and with his claims
to the vast sum of two hundred million francs accumulated from
his Civil List, as well as with landed property. He left his weapons,
his saddles and his books to his son, and he was generous to his
entourage. But the point of his Will was political. He had told
Bertrand, 'I am glad I have no religion. It is a great consolation
I have no imaginary fears. I do not fear the future'; but officially
he declared that he died a Catholic and a Frenchman and willed
that his body be interred 'by the banks of the Seine'. He was
magnanimous about nearly everyone, even his family; but he
drew the line at the rulers of England. He knew that he was dying
of the illness that had killed his father at thirty-six, but he
dictated, 'I die prematurely assassinated by the English oligarchy
and its hired killer [Lowe]. The English nation', he prophesied
hopefully, 'will not be slow to avenge me.'

By now there were four doctors in attendance and, mercifully,
their combined wisdom killed him. On 2 May they administered a
colossal dose of Mercurious Chloride (*Calomel*) a corrosive dis-
infectant, which produced hideous effects. Napoleon was now
delirious; his last coherent words *'France, Armée, Tête d'Armée'*;

212

EXTRACT FROM THE WILL OF THE EMPEROR NAPOLEON

Preserved in the Prerogative Office, Doctor's Commons, London

Ce aujourd'hui 15 avril 1821 à Longwood isle de St. hélène. — Je meure dans la Religion Apostolique et Romaine dans le sein de laquelle je suis né il y a plus de cinquante ans. Je desire que mes cendres reposent sur les bords de la Seine au milieu de ce peuple Français que j'ai tant aimé.

This present 15th of April 1821 at Longwood, island of St Helena. I die in the Holy Roman Catholic faith, in the bosom of which I was born, more than fifty years ago. I desire that my remains may be deposited on the banks of the Seine, in the midst of the French people whom I have so much loved.

Ceci est mon testament écrit tout entier de ma propre main.

This is my will written entirely with my own hand.

Signatures attached to the Will

The Empress Josephine when at Strasbourg in 1809.

Adieu mon cher Lavalette je n'ai que le tems de vous assurer de mon attachement.

Adieu my dear Lavalette I have only time to assure you of my attachment. Josephine

Marie Louise

The Empress Maria Louisa as Regent when Napoleon was at Moscow.

When Commandant of Artillery in 1793.

then, in a final animal convulsion, he leaped from his bed with such strength that Montholon, who caught him, was thrown and held down. But the legend that there was a great storm at his passing, like that before Cromwell's death, is not substantiated by the logs of the ships then at or near St Helena. On 5 May 1821, Napoleon died peacefully, his now emaciated profile showing a classic beauty, as in youth. He was fifty-one.

He was buried, with as much solemnity and pomp as practicable, in a stone-lined, rat-proof grave under the willows by a spring in Geranium Valley which had supplied his table, his coffin draped for the procession with a cloak he had worn at Marengo, and on it his sword. As it was lowered, a fusillade rang out and the salutes of the fort and the ships in the harbour echoed from the hills. Since Montholon demanded that the big slab on the tomb should be inscribed 'Napoléon', and Lowe 'Napoléon Bonaparte', it was left blank.

OPPOSITE Napoleon dictating his memoirs to Baron Gaspard Gourgaud on the island of St Helena. Gourgaud must have been an infuriating companion for Napoleon with his unpredictable temperament, but his memoirs are perhaps the most valuable.

10
Napoleon
in
World History

He started it.
W. H. AUDEN, on Napoleon

IN TERMS OF MODERN EUROPEAN HISTORY Auden's verdict seems just. Napoleon first mobilized a whole nation for war, exploited the *élan* of the French Revolution and deliberately created for himself a vast popular charisma. In the eye of the neo-classical despot is the glare of the demagogue power-maniac, who claims, as would Hitler, to embody the will of his people and commands the police, conscription and propaganda that keep them in line. And no one before had a technology behind him that could turn out cannon by the thousand to blast anything before them in battles fought by half a million men. Compared with the feats of modern dictators, Napoleon's devastations were limited; for he had no tanks, aircraft or rockets; but his conscript armies swept over whole countries, and in some lastingly transformed their social order. Julius Caesar had made a far more lasting conquest and brought barbaric peoples into civilization, but his armies technically so far surpassed those of the Iron Age Celts or Teutons that the contest had been unequal, comparable to the colonial wars of the nineteenth century. Constantine and Charlemagne had dominated huge areas, and Charles v had tried to maintain a continental hegemony; but in the European setting, Napoleon 'started it' on a modern scale.

Outside Europe he has more competitors. Alexander brought a Hellenistic way of life to the great and sophisticated Persian Empire from Egypt to northern India; Muhammad launched the desert Arabs into conquests that would transform men's lives from Morocco to Indonesia and the Philippines and over huge expanses of Africa, and he founded a new religion; a feat to which even Napoleon did not aspire. Genghis Khan and his descendants ranged over the whole of China and vast areas of central Asia and the Middle East and, after their original massacres and destruction, established a tributary *Pax Mongolica*; Timur Lenk overran the Turkish Empire and Egypt, as well as huge territories in central Asia and northern India; Babūr founded the Mughal Empire and Akbar ruled much longer over territories larger than western Europe; while the dominions of the Emperor T'ai-Tsu, founder of the Ming dynasty in the late fourteenth century, and of the Emperor Sheng-Tzu, founder of the Manchu empire in the seventeenth, dominated larger areas, and the hegemony of the later Manchus extended from Mongolia and Manchuria to Tibet and Nepal and sometimes over Burma and Indo-China.

But no one before had mastered peoples who were themselves

PREVIOUS PAGES Appiani's drawing of Napoleon the political General, sketched in 1796 after the battle of Lodi.

OPPOSITE The First Consul reviewing troops, painted by Gros.

218

through superior technology, organization and sea-power the potential rulers of the whole world, and so glimpsed the prospect of world empire. But its price was the subjugation or the alliance of the British, and here Napoleon and Hitler both failed. Napoleon's conquest of western continental and central Europe was nonetheless of world import in a new way, since what happened in Europe now concerned all mankind, leading in our own century to wars fought literally for global domination. Napoleon was the first, as Hitler was the most recent, European dictator to attempt it.

Further, save for the religious fanatics, most previous conquerors had been out to dominate the world more than to change it. Napoleon was an eighteenth-century cosmopolitan who wanted to rationalize and reform, sweep away traditional hierarchies and throw careers open to talent; he was the first great conqueror who believed in the unusual and modern idea of progress. He intended to enhance the lives of his subjects, not just to order and exploit them; and while he cynically employed the old religious and dynastic cults to sustain his power, he remained a Voltairean rationalist, watching himself with a sometimes ironic detachment. Being an outsider and an adventurer, he relished his fabulous achievements with an artist's or conductor's perception; for unlike most military conquerors, he was an intellectual – a born writer and phrase-maker, dramatizing himself. As such, he loathed and feared the common people, and though fearless in battle, lost his will and courage before civilian violence. Like Alexander, the conqueror whom he most admired and who was perhaps, in an alien context, the most like him in brilliance of mind, Napoleon wanted to construct; and in a technologically superior civilization actually to improve.

In the traditional phrase, he was thus certainly a 'man of destiny', for such people emerge when personality and the tides of change come together and men appear over life size. This Napoleon did, for he projected the unlimited violence implied in the relationships of sovereign states in Europe into a new dimension. Since the collapse of the great cosmopolitan institutions of medieval Christendom in the fourteenth century, the sovereign dynastic states had been competing with one another. Religious conflict and desire for colonies had enhanced the competition, but eighteenth-century wars were still fought with small professional armies, and on a limited scale. What Tocqueville called the ancient Public Law of Europe had remained a salutary convention, nor did one power seek utterly to destroy another.

With the French Revolution the European hierarchy itself was challenged, and the centralized nation state became something more popular, dynamic, efficient and compact. Napoleon belonged to the old order; but he was borne up by and exploited this new force which climaxed the development of sovereign territorial powers: the dynastic state had become the centralized nation with much more intransigent aims. Far from promoting the brotherhood of man, the Revolution had created a nation in arms and made new classes politically conscious, not least of the opportunities of war. Napoleon vulgarized its glamour, so that even the bourgeoisie fell for it. As after Beethoven in music, so after Napoleon in politics, things could never be the same; and this aggression, directed by Napoleon, in turn provoked other popular nationalisms, as in Germany. This movement, blended with a deeper, more ancient and widespread hatred of foreigners, as in Russia and Spain, and with the insular defiance of Great Britain, proved too much for Napoleon. When, following their tenacious purpose, the representatives of the old order, of whom Pitt had been the most determined and Talleyrand was the most sagacious, combined to restore the eighteenth-century-style balance of power, they succeeded surprisingly well: but beneath this balance of interest, popular nationalism would now develop; idealistic and liberal, as with Mazzini, militaristic, as with Fichte and Treitschke.

So Napoleon, who wanted an 'enlightened' European empire with its titles drawn from all over the Continent, roused forces which at once bore him up and which he could not control. The vision of European empire faded before the eyes of the new Charlemagne: he had been defeated not so much by the kings and the oligarchies, as by the peoples, resentful of French domination. The nation state was to be the political force of the future, not cosmopolitan empire, and it would reach its logical climax and fate in the world wars of the twentieth century. Only after that could the European peoples, chastened after disaster and eclipse, shorn of their colonial empires and of a world domination which had passed beyond them to the super powers, accept a cosmopolitan, economic and even political union of Europe.

Napoleon thus appears as the daemonic embodiment both of eighteenth-century rationalism and of the Revolution. The great disturber who swept away the old boundaries and much of the old social order, but whose purpose of European and consequent world domination failed, overcome both by established and

Napoleon the Destroyer:
a German cartoon illustrating
contemporary European
feeling towards the Emperor
in 1813.
The symbols are allegorical:
his hat represents the French
Eagle, 'maimed and crouching'
after the defeat at Leipzig;
his face is composed of
corpses; the Red Sea encircles
his throat, 'a reminder of his
drowned hosts'; the epaulette
is a hand leading the Rhenish
Confederation symbolized by
a Cobweb; and the Spider
represents the vigilant Allies
who 'have inflicted on that
Hand a deadly Sting!'

popular resistance and by extra-European, oceanic and Eurasian forces too strong even for him. Those who take the sword are apt to perish by it; and though briefly a great statesman, he began and ended as a military adventurer. But he was more than that: a butcher, of course – that was his metier – and a colossal egoist; yet a man of great vision, of brilliant and versatile personality and with that flair, force and indefatigable industry which in any sphere of life, for good or ill, we call genius.

Further Reading

Bainville, Jacques, *Napoleon* (London 1935)
Bruun, Geoffrey, in *New Cambridge Modern History*, Vol. 9 (new edition 1968)
Cronin, V., *Napoleon* (London 1971)
Cobb, Richard, *Reactions to the French Revolution*, (Oxford 1972)
  The Police and The People, Popular Protest, 1789-1820 (Oxford 1972)
Duff-Cooper, A., *Talleyrand* (London 1932)
Geyl, Pieter, *Napoleon For and Against* (London 1949)
Godechot, Jacques, *New Cambridge Modern History*, Vol. 9
  Les Institutions de la France sous la Révolution et l'Empire
    (new edition 1968)
Hardy, Thomas, *The Dynasts*
Herold, J. Christopher, *Bonaparte in Egypt* (London 1962)
  The Mind of Napoleon (New York 1955)
Holland-Rose, J., *Napoleon* (London 1902)
Howard, J. E., *Letters and Documents of Napoleon* (London 1969)
Knapton, E. J., *Empress Josephine* (Harvard 1964)
Lefebvre, J., *Napoléon (in Peuples et Civilization)* (Paris 1935)
Longford, E., *Wellington, The Years of the Sword* (London 1969)
Maccunn, J., *The Contemporary English View of Napoleon* (London 1914)
Manceron, Claude, *Which Way to Turn? Napoleon's Last Choice*, trans.
    J. Richardson (London 1961)
Markham, Felix, *Napoleon* (London 1963)
Masson, Frederic, *Napoléon Raconté par Lui-même* (Paris 1912)
  Napoléon Chez-Lui, La Journée de l'Empereur (Paris 1894)
Rosebery, Lord, *Napoleon, the Last Phase* (London 1928)
Seignobos, Charles, *A History of the French People*, trans. C. A. Phillips
    (London 1933)
Thompson, J. M., *Napoleon Bonaparte, His Rise and Fall* (London 1952)
Tolstoy, Leo, *War and Peace*, trans. L. and A. Maude (London 1957)
Turquan, J., *Napoléon Amoureux*

Sources

The basic sources are: *Correspondence de Napoléon* (28 volumes)
    1858–69, and *Oeuvres de Napoléon à Sainte Hélène* (4 volumes) 1870
Bourgeat, J., editor, *Lettres à Joséphine* (Paris 1941)
Thompson, J. M., *Napoleon's Letters* (Oxford 1929)

Memoirs

Abrantès, Duchesse d', *Memoirs* (London 1929)
Beauharnais, Eugène de, *Mémoires* (Paris 1858-60)
Bertrand, Henri-Gratien, *Cahiers de Ste Helene* (Paris 1949-59)
Caulaincourt, Armand de, *Memoirs* (London 1935)
Fouché, Joseph, *Memoirs*, ed. L. Madelin (Paris 1945)

List of Illustrations

Contents page, from left to right: Appiani's portrait of Napoleon, *Federico Arborio Mella*. Swords given to Napoleon in Egypt and used by him at Mont Thasor, photograph by Bulloz. Isabey's portrait of Josephine, *Mansell Collection*. Death of Enghien, photograph by BULLOZ. Napoleon as Emperor by Gérard, photograph by BULLOZ, *Musée National du Château de Malmaison*. The French before Moscow, lithograph by Faber du Faure, photograph by Roger-Viollet, *Bibliothèque Nationale*. Wellington, painted by Guttmann, *Radio Times Hulton Picture Library*. Napoleon's grave, *Radio Times Hulton Picture Library*.

227

228

213 Extracts from Napoleon's will, *Radio Times Hulton Picture Library*
214 Napoleon's tomb, *Radio Times Hulton Picture Library*
216 Napoleon, *Federico Arborio Mella*
219 Napoleon reviewing troops, photograph by BULLOZ, *Musée National du Château de Malmaison*
222 Napoleon, a contemporary cartoon, photograph by ARTHUR BRINICOMBE

The maps of Napoleon's campaigns in northern Italy and in Russia and Poland on pages 52–3 and pages 158–9 were drawn by Design Practitioners Ltd from those printed in *The Campaigns of Napoleon* by David Chandler, and published by The Macmillan Company, New York, 1966. The originals were drawn by Sheila Waters from preliminary drafts prepared by the author. The battle sketch diagrams of Austerlitz and Waterloo on pages 112 and 190 were also drawn by Design Practitioners Ltd, in part from references originally produced for *Summaries of Selected Military Campaigns*, 1961, published by the Department of History, United States Military Academy, West Point.

Endpapers: Rugendus's painting of the battle of Jena fought in October 1806, photograph by BULLOZ, *Bibliothèque du Musée de l'Armée*

Picture research by Christopher Maddock.

Index

230